A CHANGE FOR THE BETTER

COMPANION BOOK FOR PARTNERS AND FAMILIES OF PARTICIPANTS ENGAGING IN A DOMESTIC AND FAMILY VIOLENCE INTERVENTION PROGRAM

AMANDA AKERS

First published by Ultimate World Publishing 2024
Copyright © 2024 Amanda Akers

ISBN

Paperback: 978-1-923255-65-4
Ebook: 978-1-923255-66-1

Amanda Akers has asserted her rights under the Copyright, Designs and Patents Act 1988 to be identified as the author of this work. The information in this book is based on the author's experiences and opinions. The publisher specifically disclaims responsibility for any adverse consequences which may result from use of the information contained herein. Permission to use information has been sought by the author. Any breaches will be rectified in further editions of the book.

All rights reserved. No part of this publication may be reproduced, stored in or introduced into a retrieval system, or transmitted in any form, or by any means (electronic, mechanical, photocopying, recording or otherwise) without the prior written permission of the author. Any person who does any unauthorised act in relation to this publication may be liable to criminal prosecution and civil claims for damages. Enquiries should be made through the publisher.

Cover design: Ultimate World Publishing
Layout and typesetting: Ultimate World Publishing
Editor: James Salmon

Ultimate World Publishing
Diamond Creek,
Victoria Australia 3089
www.writeabook.com.au

DEDICATION

To the women who are giving their partners
or family members
another chance to make
a change for the better.

CONTENTS

Dedication	iii
Introduction	1
Chapter 1: Your First Chapter	5
Chapter 2: His Next Chapter	19
Chapter 3: Rebuilding Trust, One Group Session at a Time	31
Chapter 4: Thoughts, Feelings and Behaviours	39
Chapter 5: What Do You Believe?	47
Chapter 6: What Did He Believe?	55
Chapter 7: Where's the Respect?	63
Chapter 8: Can it Really Get Better?	71
Chapter 9: Children Matter	83
Chapter 10: Doing it Together: Same Level…Equal	91
Chapter 11: Actually Talking	95
Chapter 12: What if He Relapses?	105
Afterword	113
About the Author	115
Amanda as a Guest Speaker	117

INTRODUCTION

This book is for women whose partner, husband, or family member is commencing, or has commenced, a men's behaviour change program for addressing their domestic and family violence.

As a health professional co-facilitating men's behaviour change programs, it became apparent that while men are attending their behaviour change program, women could feel in limbo, lost, or longing for information about what their partner or family member is doing. She could be asking herself: What should a woman expect in terms of change? When should she see change in her partner? What if he doesn't change? What if he believes he's changing, but she doesn't? How can she trust the process of change? Why does he get the attention in a group, and she has to stay at home alone or with the children?

Some men are good at communicating what occurs for them in the group, but other men, not necessarily through their own fault, are not so good at talking after their group attendance. This can be for a number of reasons, a common one being that they may have had to be awake early to start work and had a long hectic day, then attended a night group. When they arrive home after the group session they may be tired and find it difficult to communicate about the group experience and what they've learned.

Instead of women repeatedly asking "How was the group?", and repeatedly hearing "Fine" as a response, this book provides female partners some more specific information about the process of the group. It is designed to help women ask more specific questions that relate to their own queries about the process, and help them to learn what changes to expect in their partner as they progress through the behaviour change curriculum. In a nutshell, this book should enhance communication between women and their male partners or family members who are attending the behaviour change group.

The aim of this book is to ensure that women are not left in the dark during the behaviour change program, that they have specific information, and can maintain control over their lives. It allows them to follow the changes that should be made, and strategies that are taught, to prevent future violence and keep them and their children safe, after having experienced domestic and family violence.

It is expected that, at some time during the behaviour change program, women may be interested in what occurs in the group sessions, and how they can engage in conversations about the program with their partner or family member between group sessions. Women may start to feel more connected to the program, rather than having to wait until their partner or family member tells them about the group. This book is designed to encourage openness and discussion, listening and understanding, and promote equality and non-violence.

After domestic and family violence occurs, there's usually been police attendance, statements given, court attendance, an interview

INTRODUCTION

for acceptance into the behaviour change program, a phone call to the female partner or family member, and a general upheaval of family life, not to mention the domestic and family violence incidents themselves. Women are often given information about domestic and family violence before and during the court proceedings, and informed about what constitutes domestic and family violence, or they may have researched it themselves. The man goes off to the behaviour change program, meets with the facilitators and meets other men. He can talk, contribute, and engage with others. For the woman, the support can seem to stop, almost as though the focus moves to the man and stays there. He is focused on the group, and on himself. She may have to help him get to the group on time, or even drive him there.

Reading this book is a way for women to stay engaged during the long behaviour change process, to re-read the book if their focus wanes, to stay informed, and it is a way for men to share the experience with their female partner, so she remains on his level, not above or below.

Disclaimer
NOTE: Behaviour change programs for people in same-sex relationships, or for female perpetrators, are slightly different from programs for men in heterosexual relationships, hence their partners will benefit from a similar book addressing their specific programs.

CHAPTER 1
YOUR FIRST CHAPTER

Through constant familiarity, we can definitely establish new behaviour patterns, using our tendency to form habits to our advantage. If we make a steady effort, we can overcome any form of negative conditioning and make positive changes in our lives. But we need to remember that genuine change doesn't happen overnight.

— *Dalai Lama*

Congratulations! Your partner, or family member is attending a domestic and family violence intervention program, otherwise known as a Men's Behaviour Change Program, and it may be that you helped him get to this stage of his attendance. Over the next 20 or more weeks, depending on the program your partner may be in, you're going to get two hours a week all to yourself while he's away in his group program doing work on himself. He may be fulfilling his court orders, or an agreement he may have with a solicitor or with you or with the extended family. He'll be learning to be accountable for his domestic and family violence.

Over the coming weeks, and definitely by the end of the program, the violence that's been occurring in your life should reduce. Hopefully, he bought this book for you, so you're a part of this program, by having information about what he's learning. It's important for you to feel that your experience is being addressed, and in the Duluth Domestic and Family Violence Intervention Program, the female (who is usually the victim) is consistently acknowledged in the training room when the male participants are talking. It is the co-facilitators' jobs to ensure that, wherever possible, your experience is acknowledged, or there is an attempt to acknowledge what you experienced, so it isn't brushed over. We want to make sure that the men in these intervention programs are thinking about the women they've abused, and not just thinking about themselves.

The facilitators will be asking the men to share examples of what has happened between the two of you, or other family members, and then asking them to reflect on how that may have been for you. Not to punish them but to encourage them to keep a focus on why they're there, and acknowledge that it's not all about them. It includes you, and affects your life in so many ways.

Why do I say the men? The Domestic and Family Violence statistics show that men are predominantly the perpetrators of violence and that women are predominantly the victims. Health data shows that women present to the Emergency Departments of the hospitals for injuries more often than men. But we're not only addressing physical and sexual violence in this program, we're also addressing coercive control which can lead to physical or sexual violence.

YOUR FIRST CHAPTER

It's an important time to note all the times he may have told you to "go and get help", or "go and learn something". Guess what he's doing now? This is now him taking an opportunity to practice what he's been preaching. He's going to have to address some of the comments he may have made and acknowledge that those comments can be hurtful.

The main aim of this program is not about the men. It's about the women, the victims, and this may be you. The men's behaviour change program is all about keeping you safe. By now, you should have contact from one of the facilitators or the women's advocates of the program. If this hasn't happened yet, please start asking why, and get answers. All men's behaviour change programs should have a women's advocate and if you're still in the relationship with your partner and you haven't been contacted yet, even by one of the co-facilitators, you should have been. Perhaps your partner can ask why at his next group session.

It is vitally important, if you are still in the relationship with your partner, that you're safe while he's undertaking this group program, and that you feel you have someone whom you can speak with outside of the program, but also from within the program if you'd like – this may be the women's advocate. If your partner is not doing the Betterment Program with Akers Psychology, the program your partner is doing is likely to have a women's advocate attached to the program.

Getting started

Your partner is going to start learning how to become accountable for his past domestic violence by replacing violence with non-violence and non-threatening behaviour. If he doesn't, you may need to re-think the relationship.

A CHANGE FOR THE BETTER

You may have noticed that on the cover of this book, the man is leaving the house and the female is standing at the door waving to him. Throughout the course of reading this book and throughout the program that your partner is attending, the woman at the door may be you. You may be waving to your partner as he leaves in the car or by public transport to attend his group program.

Hopefully, your partner has bought this book for you, which symbolises that he's keeping you in mind, and that he is doing something for you while he's also doing something for himself and keeping society safe. This book is a gesture for you, and information for you, symbolising that you're part of this program. Part of the program means keeping you in the room and in the mind of your partner.

If you bought this book for yourself, be aware that you will mentioned with respect in the conversations that we have throughout the program.

This first chapter is the longest in the book and it might be the most important for you. If you can get through it, the rest of the chapters will be easy to read. If you find at any time the information in this chapter or even this book is difficult for you, put it down. You can pick it up later on when you're in a better frame of mind to read it. Readers are likely to be at different stages of their journey with domestic violence in their relationship. Go with what feels right for you. Remember that this book is a gesture from your partner to show that he wants you involved in the relationship, which now includes his journey in a group program, and this book can be something you can both use as a discussion theme for positive conversations.

In Australia to date, these groups typically run for 20 weeks. In the USA these group programs run for 27 weeks, and some can run for up to 12 months duration. At the time of writing this book Australia had begun introducing the 27-week programs. It seems like a long time to attend a group, but it has been shown through extensive research that it takes a long time to change the beliefs and thought processes that families and society have encouraged and supported for some men to feel entitled to abuse their partners. It therefore takes a long time to 'unlearn' these beliefs and thought processes.

So how are you going to see this 'unlearning' happen? What are you going to see as your partner starts this group program? Maybe not a lot in the first few weeks, or maybe he's excited and feels he's learning something early on. He might also be finding it a chore in the beginning – after all, it may not have been his choice to join the group program. For some people, the real learning can happen towards the end of the program, when all parts of the program start to fit together and gel in their mind.

What is domestic and family violence?

Domestic and family violence is physical or sexual violence that occurs in a relationship with a romantic or live-in partner, or violence against a family member: parent; child; sibling; or other relative. It includes violence that occurs in the presence of a child or other relative, as witnessing violence can also have long-term effects on the observer.

My partner isn't in a men's behaviour change program yet

If your partner isn't in a men's behaviour change program yet, has he engaged in domestic and family violence? Has he been charged with assault, had a domestic violence, or interim order taken out against him? Has he been charged with sexual violence or assault?

If your partner or family member has ever hit, pushed, shoved, scratched, burned, or hurt you in any way, and you're still not sure if he needs to attend a men's behaviour change group, ask yourself these questions about your partner's use of violence, as posed in Lunday Bancroft's book:

- Has he ever trapped you in a room and not let you out?
- Has he ever raised a fist as if he were going to hit you?
- Has he ever thrown an object that hit you or nearly did?
- Has he ever held you down or grabbed you to restrain you?
- Has he ever threatened to hurt you?

"If the answer to any of these questions is yes, then we can stop wondering whether he'll ever be violent; he already has been."
Lundy Bancroft

In Australia, the laws have recently changed around coercive control. This is because when violence has occurred and an investigation of incidents and actions leading up to the violence is made, coercive control has usually been present in the history of the relationship. The statistics show that coercive control appears before violence, but is often over-looked.

What is coercive control?

Coercive control can occur almost silently alongside physical or sexual violence, and can be experienced by the female partner as:

- intimidation
- humiliation
- exploitation
- regulation
- isolation
- micromanagement in everyday life

Both domestic violence and coercive control have an underlying ideology relating to the history of male dominance and control. In his book 'Coercive Control' Evan Stark describes coercive control as being used to reduce women's ability to make gains, manage women's activities in and around the home, hinder their access to support, reduce their ability to reflect on their lives, and maintain dependence on their male partner.

Historically, women have been expected to have a commitment to domestic duties and retain the stereotype of gender roles, where women predominantly attend to child-raising and domestic chores, while men bring in a higher wage and perform tasks such as lawn mowing and minor repairs to the home, with men engaging in no more than 20-30% of domestic chores (Stark, E 2007).

Over the years, the search for equality for women has increased as women sought positions of employment or careers, which could jeopardise men's dominance and traditional male privilege. Coercive control is used to maintain women in a subordinate, or in some cases even servant-like, role. Over time, if coercive control doesn't work, it could result in physical or sexual violence, as a reminder to the woman that the male is in control.

More recently, women have come to experience more equality in their ability to earn money from employment and careers, find independence rather than remain dependent on their partners, achieve rights, resources, cultural autonomy, and legal and political equality. This has encouraged many men to accept women's equality and to make a compromise to their sense of male privilege. It also makes men who use coercive control a minority, quite out of order, and more of a focus as perpetrators of domestic and family violence.

Society has supported the notion of male privilege in the past, but as society is slowly advancing to support the safety of women, the need to encourage men to make a change for the better must not be neglected. It's one thing to make women safe, but we can't ignore the actions that have occurred to make them feel unsafe. Some men have learned to use male privilege and violence, but they can unlearn it.

If you're still not sure about whether your partner needs to 'unlearn' some of his actions, call Akers Psychology and have a talk with us about your situation. It may help make your choices and decisions clearer.

What you can do if your partner is in a men's behaviour change group?

If you've made the choice to stay in the relationship with your partner, and he's attending a men's behaviour change group, you may not see too much change in the short term. I'd encourage you to observe his actions, see what he's doing after the first week, after the second week, and continue to see how things are going as he progresses through the sessions. Don't have your expectations up too high at the start. Try to listen and talk with him, if you're at that point in your relationship.

YOUR FIRST CHAPTER

For some of you, it may be hard for you to trust you partner at this stage, so just observe. Receiving or reading this book doesn't mean you have to trust him just yet, but it means that you're a part of the journey and that you want to know what's occurring. If you happen to have a partner who's not great at telling you about his day or his experience, that doesn't mean you can't ask him about it. You could ask him to tell you one thing he learned, or one thing he shared in the group. Some men are good at sharing and some are not.

One of the requirements of the program is that men share their experiences. If you feel up to it, compliment him on his progress. It doesn't necessarily have to be a great, overly positive compliment, but something simple like "That's good"; "I'm glad you went"; or "Sounds good", just to give him a bit of encouragement. If you feel you can. Some women find it hard to give compliments after domestic violence has occurred, but may do this later on when they see more significant change or when there's been a significant period of time with no violence, no coercive control, and more positive experiences in their relationship.

Keeping you safe

In relation to keeping you safe, this program is not about avoiding what's going on. Your partner will have signed a contract stating that he will not engage in any violence or acts of violence while he attends the program. The fact he's in the program does not excuse any violence, so there shouldn't be any relapses to violence. This program does not support violence or relapses.

If your partner does relapse and use violence towards you, it's likely you'll need help to decide what to do. Make contact with the person with whom you feel most safe contacting. If he relapses during the course of the program, you need to be safe in the first instance. You'll have a safety plan to help you through the violence.

The co-facilitators need to be informed of the threatening or violent behaviour. They will ascertain if your partner is suitable to remain in the program. If he's engaged with probation and parole or bail conditions or GBB, this may be reported as a breach of probation or parole, especially if your partner has been court-ordered or bailed to the program, as this is a legal situation. This is still breaking the law, as is breaching a contract or a court order. Please let us know if there's a relapse. He is not in this program to continue any violence or controlling actions towards you.

You may be thinking to yourself, why do I have this book? It's not about me, it's about him. Well, this program is all about you. It's about your choice to remain in a relationship where there has been coercive control or domestic and family violence.

You may be thinking to yourself, it's not about me learning, it's about him learning. He's attending the men's behaviour change program and we need to keep the focus on him, but the aim for behaviour change is to keep women safe, reduce the violence or control at a relationship level, and at a family level, to get family members to realise it's not ok for women and children to be treated this way, or observe others being treated this way. It's also at society level that we need to see change, and encourage groups and governments to accept that any sort of violence or threats towards women are unacceptable.

Another question may relate to how the co-facilitators will know what he does between his group sessions. Co-facilitators are there with him during the group session, and won't necessarily know what's happening for you between group times. This is why, if anything is happening to you, you should talk with someone, such as the women's advocate. Not necessarily the co-facilitators, but you can contact them as well if you wish. If you change your mind about being in the relationship, or anything else about the relationship, offences, court order, communication, or incidents it would be a good idea to talk about it with someone who can help you through what has occurred for you and to discuss what could occur for your partner. We may not know unless he relays it to the group.

How will the co-facilitators know what he does between sessions?

He will be with the co-facilitators for 1½ to 2 hours, and then he goes home to you. There are no cameras on the wall, they don't know what occurs at home so if something negative is happening, only you will be able to tell someone what is occurring. If there's behaviour that's not acceptable, if you're not comfortable or safe, if you've changed your mind about him, if any violent, abusive, or controlling behaviours are occurring, or he's not communicating with you positively, or not at all, then someone needs to know so you can be supported.

The co-facilitators are not going to know unless he discloses it in the group, or you relay it to them or the women's advocate. You should have someone to talk with, to discuss your options or your safety plan.

What is a safety plan?

A safety plan is a plan for your safety, if your partner becomes violent again. This is vitally important as men can become more violent at the end of a relationship or if he believes you're about to leave the relationship.

A safety plan is usually developed with someone such as a women's advocate or someone from a domestic and family violence service or hotline. It will include making a plan for you to leave, manage the children and your pets, and involves your safety after you have left. There will be a checklist to work through, and even tips on what to pack if you're leaving the house.

If your partner is not violent again you won't need a safety plan, but it's better to have one in place because if there is more violence your mind will be pre-occupied with staying safe, not developing a safety plan at the last minute.

What is a women's advocate?

A women's advocate is a female who can support you and listen to you. She is not a co-facilitator of the men's behaviour change group. She will be objective and focused on you and your safety. An advocate is a person who represents another person's best interests. They may support or speak on behalf of the other person. A women's advocate understands domestic and family violence and coercive control and she works with the female victims of domestic and family violence and can assist to action a woman's safety plan if required.

You may be thinking "This is all too much!" or that this group is acting as another stressor for you. You may just want him to be a better man, husband, partner, or friend, or you may not want to think about the group. That's great that you want him to be better, and the co-facilitators in the program want that too, but they want you to be safe. That's the most important focus. The facilitators of the program will try to help him to learn to be accountable and learn how to respond and communicate respectfully, and if they

YOUR FIRST CHAPTER

achieve it then they're doing a good job, but it still takes time. It doesn't happen overnight.

Some of the things you can do to feel a part of the program are:

- Look at the group topics that he'll be talking and learning about.
- See what the words are that they're using to describe things in the program.
- Be familiar with the content of the program.
- Ask your partner what the theme or the topic was for the group they just attended.
- Ask your partner if they shared some of their information in the group or whether they joined in with the small break-out group.
- Ask your partner if they talked about a particular topic that's of interest to you, it might be something that's non-verbal or non-physical.
- Check out the flyer he's been given.
- Try to talk with him about the themes in the program.

Make sure you have contact numbers for the co-facilitators of the group, and the contact number for the women's advocate. There are also other useful numbers you may need for yourself.

Betterment Domestic and Family Violence Intervention Program at Akers Psychology 07 5519 9668 or

000 or Local Police Station
Your Women's Advocate's contact details
Women's Refuge
Women's Housing
Child Safety

A CHANGE FOR THE BETTER

Alcohol and Other Drugs rehabs, out-patient services, inpatient detox units
Women's Groups
Parenting Programs

CHAPTER 2

HIS NEXT CHAPTER

The secret of change is to focus all of your energy not on fighting the old, but on building the new.
— *Socrates*

Whilst this may be your first chapter, with your partner finally agreeing, or being ordered, to attend a domestic and family violence intervention program, this is his next chapter. His chapter needs to be a chapter about change, not playing the 'blame/shame game' and blaming others for his actions or words, or making others feel ashamed. His next chapter must be about changing for the better.

When you both first met each other, and there were no negative behaviours, things were rosy, you were falling in love, enjoying each other's company, engaging in positive activities - pleasurable activities. The next chapter for both of you should be getting as close

A CHANGE FOR THE BETTER

as possible to how things were at the start of your relationship. A lot has changed and it may be inconceivable for you to imagine at this stage that this should be a goal that he has to rekindle, back to where your relationship was in the beginning. While you may not be feeling that you trust him to get there, or you may not trust the process, one of his key objectives should be re-establishing the trust and being mindful of the fact that you may not trust him, so he needs to earn your trust again.

Keeping your family together, keeping two parents for the children, can be a common goal that you both may want. It can be one of the reasons women choose to stay in a relationship: so they can maintain another parent to help raise the children; sharing the income to make the costs of having a family more manageable; sharing the workload - domestic chores; engaging in parenting to make managing the costs of child care easier; and being good role models for the children. Seeing the scenarios where children may take examples of parenting into their own parenting behaviour when they become adults, suggests that positive behaviour change can be important for both you, your children, and even your grandchildren.

Your partner's next chapter must involve working on the present and the future. The present being right now, today. The fact that he's started this program is a positive; encouraging you to be involved and to understand information about the program, taking it one day at a time and trying to show you that he cares enough to make some change, and wants you to trust him, both now and for the future so there will be a future for this relationship and for your family.

HIS NEXT CHAPTER

Scenario 1. Early Changes

Nate attended the first session of his behaviour change program with an anxious feeling. He was still stirred up from being in court. He'd never been charged for anything before and now he had an assault charge and a domestic violence order (DVO) that had to be changed to allow him back in the house with his partner and children. He was glad he wasn't in jail.

As soon as Nate saw the other men, the posters on the wall, the two co-facilitators whom he'd already met at his assessment appointment, he tried to relax. When he started hearing the other men's stories he was surprised at their situations, their charges, their repeat offending, and he told himself he was never going to be violent with his partner, Natalia, again. He decided to listen up. He accepted that he needed to be there. He was so close to losing his partner and his kids. He'd had to live with his parents until the DVO was changed, and while he didn't like being told what to do, or how to act with his family, he knew he had to. Nate is one of the lucky ones. As Nate proceeded through the program, he found he was getting those 'light-bulb' moments almost every session. He was learning something new, another way to see Natalia's side of living with him, and how he'd treated her, and how he could improve.

Scenario 2.

Jackson started the program with some resistance. He didn't want to be there, but he didn't want to be in jail. He sat down, folded his arms and didn't say much for the first few sessions. He admitted that he didn't think he'd done anything that other men don't do, and he believed his partner had taunted him and attacked him. He was stuck with the thoughts that she'd hit him first.

A CHANGE FOR THE BETTER

Jackson worked long hours and had limited information to contribute most sessions, so the co-facilitators spent time working with him to ensure he contributed each session. They tried to focus on his shared information, at times asking others what they might do instead, or what others thought about aspects of Jackson's interactions with his partner.

Jackson didn't really care what they thought. He was focused on his own situation. He believed that he knew what he knew. His partner, Olivia, was still with him. He knew Olivia loved him and he felt safe in the relationship. He was sure she wouldn't leave him. Jackson was cold towards the group program most of the time. Unlike Nate, Jackson didn't take to the program in the early weeks. He just turned up and went through the motions. But the co-facilitators didn't give up on him. They showed patience and seemed to understand his presentation. After all, they'd seen it before.

During the third last week of the program, Jackson came to the group visibly agitated. He hung back from sharing until he was the last to share about his week. He nearly broke down as he told the other men in the group that Olivia had gone to stay with her parents and said she mightn't come back. Olivia had given him an ultimatum. She told him she hadn't seen any change in him. He knew she'd been talking with the women's advocate, and he became angry at the women's advocate, trying to blame her for leading Olivia away from him, and colluding with Olivia against him. At this stage, one of the men whose partner had left him when he assaulted her, spoke up and reminded Jackson that he was victim-blaming, minimising and denying his role in the situation. The participant highlighted the key aspects of what he'd learned in the program and asked Jackson if he'd been listening all through the program.

Jackson was angry and went to the kitchen, made a coffee, and returned to the group, staying silent, sulking, and sorry for himself. By the end of the group session, Jackson shared that he really listened this time. He said he needed to have a session with the psychologist between group sessions, and that he realised that he did need the group program. He admitted that he hadn't changed much and thought Olivia would never leave him, and he now knew that he was wrong, she could leave him.

By the end of Jackson's group program he was starting to get the messages being imparted in the group. He was starting to change the way he spoke to, and treated, Olivia. He chose to keep seeing the psychologist after he'd completed the program. He didn't grasp the concepts until later in the program, but he did grasp them.

Scenario 3.

Chris was a repeat offender. He'd been to jail for assaulting his ex-partner and she left him when he was charged with 'Assault occasioning bodily harm'. Chris talked of "loving women", saying that he was a "lover not a hater". Chris was court-ordered to attend the men's behaviour change program on his release as it wasn't offered in the jail. He'd started one of the programs before going to jail the previous year, but he'd started it too close to his court date and he was sentenced to jail mid-program. Chris was physically violent, especially when he was on a methamphetamine bender. He'd caused significant injuries to his previous partners. Chris had lived in several states of Australia and had friends wherever he went. None of his friends had ever questioned the way he treated his female partners. Chris wore his jail history on his sleeve as he'd done time for drug possession, dealing drugs, and stolen goods.

A CHANGE FOR THE BETTER

While Chris was in jail, he started a new relationship with Emily, who was the ex-partner of a one of Chris' friends. Emily visited Chris in jail, talked with him daily by phone, and agreed that he could live with her on his release.

When he was released, Chris moved in with Emily, feeling right at home. He celebrated his release for the first few days, partying with old friends, going out until late, and spending limited time with Emily. Within a week of his release, Chris started another relationship with a woman named Taylor. He kept both relationships going until Emily, who'd stuck by him while he was in jail, found messages to and from Taylor on Chris' phone. Chris was a well-built, good-looking man who was self-confident, self-assured, and women loved him. He knew he could get a new partner as soon as his last one or two left him, and he relished attention from women.

Chris participated in the program. He talked openly about what he'd done in his relationships, showing evidence of victim-blaming in his reports of his own behaviour towards his partners. He occasionally laughed when other men shared their stories and views on the topics of the week. The co-facilitators pulled Chris aside after the first few weeks to inform him that his laughing was inappropriate and warned him to attend to the program with a serious mind, or he may be asked to leave. The focus of the program is not only to learn from one's own behaviour but to learn from other men in the group. While Chris ceased laughing openly at others, he retained his stoic attitude, shared less about his partners of the past and the present, and was observed as being reserved and cold. He was there because he had to be there.

Unlike Nate, Chris did not report having 'light-bulb' moments, or learning ways to change. Unlike Jackson, Chris didn't even get to the end of the program. Chris didn't attend the 15th session. He had argued with, and assaulted, Emily as she was telling Chris to move out of her house. Neighbours had called the police. Chris had breached his bail, he was charged, and further bail was refused and Chris was in jail again. No change made.

Several of the men in the group Chris attended were shocked when they learned of Chris' breach of bail and his imprisonment. Several were not surprised at all. This was a reality check for the group.

Sometimes people aren't ready to change. Their beliefs and learned behaviour can be deeply entrenched. Ongoing substance use, drugs or alcohol, can interfere with learning outcomes, and certain personality issues can be a barrier to change. Such people may end up in a men's behaviour change group, but they don't go unnoticed. The co-facilitators are trained to identify men who are resistant to change or slow to change, and the other men in the group notice other men's behaviour too. After all, the group setting involves sitting in a circle, and there's nowhere to hide.

One of the reasons the men's behaviour change programs are so long (20 to 25 weeks) is that it can take time to unlearn the deeply entrenched beliefs around non-violence and non-threatening behaviour, and equality and respect. Jackson and Chris both took time to challenge their own beliefs. Jackson succeeded eventually, but Chris didn't. If the program had been any shorter, Jackson wouldn't have arrived at the time he started to accept change. Chris still might've assaulted Emily, but the impact this news had on the other men in the group would not have occurred.

A CHANGE FOR THE BETTER

How is change occurring in your relationship?

If your relationship doesn't improve, it may be a sign that your partner may not be doing some of the work. He may not be taking in the learning or the concepts of the group, especially if you are seeing the controlling or violent behaviour continuing. After all, he could be presenting his best self to the group and staying the same abusive person at home. You can certainly give him a warning, get some support for yourself. You could give him one last chance, with supports in place; however, you may not necessarily choose to do that, and that's OK. If you're not sure what to do, talk with the women's advocate, or your closest friend or family member, or all of them.

Any relapse back to violence needs to be reported so that you can get support. This may be something you consider throughout the program. You may continue to wonder if you feel that this relationship is what you want, and whether you feel he is prepared and committed to make change, to make life better for you and your family.

It may not be you standing at the door, waving him goodbye for good, it may be you waving him goodbye to go to the group, and returning to you with new found knowledge for equality, respect, and ongoing commitment.

You might have thoughts such as "Things will never be the same as they were before", and that may be the case, but they might get even better. It can be the case that when men start to make change and trust the process, communication becomes better, their mood becomes better, the time you spend together becomes better, the planning for holidays or activities becomes more positive. It's crucial that we maintain hope that things can improve, but you have to see the results.

A change for the better doesn't erase any of the domestic and family violence that has occurred, but it can produce a deeper sense of commitment or intimacy if the trust can eventually be re-established.

You may think "I'll never fully trust him ever again" and that's OK. Observe him and see where you're both at in a year or two. Just observe; trust may come, but make sure you're not pushing yourself to a point where you're not comfortable to trust, and are not keeping the relationship in limbo for years, as that's not productive for you, for him, or for the children if you have any. If you're not sure about trust, talk with the women's advocate, or a counsellor or psychologist.

Three actions that you can take as a result of reading this chapter about **his** next chapter of change:

1. Allocate a time frame. How long will you give him? Six months or a year? Will you give him until the end of the program? Tell him how long you're going to give him, so you're communicating clearly and letting him know. Make sure you tell him at a time that you're both communicating positively, so that's it's not a threat or an ultimatum or leaving him dangling on the edge, waiting to finish the program, waiting to see when your time-frame is up. It's more about the planning, so part of your planning in this process is that you'll give him, for example, six months or twelve months and you make it very clear for yourself and for him.

2. Decide if you'll give him a warning if he has a lapse in his behaviour. For some women, one lapse is not OK. One period of their partner going back to old behaviour is not

ok. For example, if he has a meltdown and starts throwing things. You need to decide if this is OK, or not OK, and only you can make this decision. For some women there is no exception and the first time he does anything abusive or controlling it's over, it's done.

3. Let him know. If you're prepared for him to have one lapse, let him know. Give him a warning: "I told you when you started this program, (or when you came back to live in the house), that if you do this again (for example shouting or name calling, not physical or sexual violence) it will be over". This is his single warning, and if he does it again, that's it, it's time for him to move out.

Special note:
Physical or sexual violence is not cause for a warning, it's not OK at all. It's cause for being expelled from the group program. It's not acceptable, as it's harm to you, it may breach his bail, he's broken his promise to you, and it breaches his contract for the men's behaviour change program, in which he agrees he will not engage in violence while he's in the group program. Children are affected, you are affected and it is against the law.

If violence occurs, he will not be allowed to return to the group, and it is not your fault. It is his behaviour, his decision, his actions.

In the case of another incident of violence it could be you standing at the doorway, waving goodbye to him like the woman on the front cover of this book. That is you, acknowledging that violence is absolutely not acceptable. In some states, territories, or countries where coercive control is a criminal offence, you may also need to consider his behaviour in relation to coercive control.

Access the women's advocate to discuss his lapse or relapse. If you're seeing behaviour that you don't like, if you're seeing behaviour and you don't quite trust it, if you're not seeing any change, those three items as seen in the scenarios: early change, late change, or no change, are behaviours for you to be monitoring. Talk with the women's advocate and discuss your thoughts and feelings.

Bounce off some of your ideas with her. Is your partner the sort of person who grasps concepts quickly? Does he learn from others or learn from himself? Does he learn through reflecting on his own behaviour, or is he one that takes time to grasp the full picture, getting it slowly but getting it eventually? Does your partner process information well? Or is he a follower? Listening to other males and repeating what they say and do?

Your partner's next chapter needs to be a positive one, one that involves change, at any pace, and one in which you can see change. Hopefully it's positive, new, and rewarding, for him and for you as well.

CHAPTER 3
REBUILDING TRUST, ONE GROUP SESSION AT A TIME

Do not accept anything as the truth if it lacks love. And do not accept anything as love which lacks truth. One without the other becomes a destructive lie.

— *Edith Stein*

When domestic and family violence occurs, boundaries are breached, and trust is broken. For those of you who are married their wedding vows are broken, for those in a relationship whether it's short or long-term, your commitment and your assumptions about safety in your relationship are violated. You, as the victim of violence, have been violated and hurt, by the person in the relationship who is supposed to protect you. How can this happen?

A CHANGE FOR THE BETTER

Rebuilding trust after violence means that you need to learn to feel safe in your relationship with your partner, particularly if that person is a man. Men have more muscle mass than women. Men are stronger, men can hurt us. We have to be able to trust our partner, trust that they will protect us and that they won't hurt us. We have to feel we are trusted. Sometimes women don't trust men. That can upset the man because he may feel that he can't trust in return. This then upsets the woman if she feels she's not seen as trustworthy and this doesn't make for a good combination. It becomes a vicious cycle. If we feel trusted, it can make it easier to trust him. Others, such as your children, need to feel safe and trusting as well, so there are no surprises in your lives or theirs. Things may not be overly predictable, but at least we shouldn't have negative surprises, things happening that might ruin our day, or that we might not have expected or appreciated.

It is a shocking truth that abuse, lies, and infidelity can all be skeletons in the closet. These actions may have happened before in your past relationships. We all know that lies hurt, they hurt us, they hurt others, sometimes they can hurt the person who's doing the lying.

It's important to identify what it means for you to feel safe. In your own home it's good to know that no-one can break in, no-one can steal your belongings, nobody can hurt you or hurt your children. When safety is breached or violence occurs in a relationship or marriage, it breaches the trust, and the boundaries are violated – the boundaries of trust, relationship, and security.

It's also important for you to identify what has to happen for that trust to be re-built. You may be thinking that if you don't trust him then he won't trust you. You might feel that you cannot trust him and that if you were to start dis-trusting him again and he knows about it, he may be less likely to trust you.

REBUILDING TRUST, ONE GROUP SESSION AT A TIME

It may be the case that it depends on the individual person – after all, we're all different. How can we encourage others to trust him? If we don't trust him and then, for example, our parents, or our best friends, don't trust him, because they see that we don't trust him, it might be hard for us to encourage them to trust him. This can make for a difficult situation if your partner seeks your support to regain your parents' trust. So if you have some trust in him, even just a little, when others are doubtful, you may be able to say a few positive words rather than engaging in negative communication every time his name is mentioned. But it has to be real.

If your partner is trying to make a change by attending this group, it'd be good to try to trust that he is trying to change, so he can get the most out of the group that he possibly can. So, one of the responses to your friends, family, or children might be that while they're not trusting him, you can remind them that he's trying to make change by attending the group, and that you're trying to trust him and you'd like their support. This is not about fully defending him but it's about stating that the evidence is that he's attempting to make a change.

If we continue to engage in lies, or if he does, then that can lead to more surprises and second-guessing behaviour, and then we start to worry. "What if he's really doing this? What if others really think he is?" We can work ourselves up into excessive worry, which can lead to anxiety, which can lead to issues with our friends and family and you're then back on the cycle of staying away from people, which looks pretty much like isolation.

Family and friends will then assume he's trying to isolate you from them, which of course, falls under coercive control. So, how do we manage this if there are lies? Do we label the person a liar? We might if the person has been caught out lying.

A CHANGE FOR THE BETTER

Typically, people who are labeled as liars don't lie all of the time. They might lie about where they've been and what they've been doing. If they fall over and hurt their wrist and go to the doctor and the doctor asks if they've injured their wrist before, they're likely to be honest so the doctor has all the information required for treatment. This suggests that people who lie don't necessarily lie all the time; there are going to be some truths. It's up to you to be able to navigate what is truth and what is a lie. Of course, if this is too difficult, or if you've already given this relationship all of your energy and this feels insurmountable, then it's back to considering whether this relationship is going to work for you.

What can you do about lying behaviours? You can role-model telling the truth, by always telling the truth, and hopefully most of us do that already. You can remind people that you're being honest and it's not difficult. We can get out of the worst situations by telling the truth. If our partner lies, they must have a remarkably good memory to recall all the lies at a later stage, whereas if they tell the truth they only have to remember what occurred, and most people can do that unless they a memory problem.

If we're concerned that our partner might be lying, look for evidence, for or against, but not too much, just one example. If, for example, your partner came home late from work, taking an hour to get home. If your partner said they came straight home from work and you know that it only takes 20 minutes for them to drive home, you could say that "Yesterday it only took you 20 minutes to drive home from work and today it took an hour". There's a piece of evidence that may suggest it's a lie, and you don't need to go away and do any detective work, as one piece of evidence is usually enough to give you an idea of whether the truth is coming out. You may just hold that in your mind. If your partner produces information about a car accident on his way home, or a traffic jam of some sort, then he has some evidence which you may need to consider.

Try to trust the process, try to trust your partner, and trust yourself. Look at one piece of information at a time so it doesn't become overwhelming.

If you can't do this, if you can't trust, if you don't want to look for evidence of lies or truths, then that's OK too. It's OK to take your time to regain trust in your partner, because the boundaries have been breached. If your partner is engaging in a domestic and family violence program, your trust has been violated and boundaries need re-building. Rest assured that he'll be encouraged to tell the truth in the group.

However long it takes for you to regain trust, that is up to you. We would hope that your partner is prepared to be patient, especially if he is hoping to be trusted by you again. If he can't wait, that's his problem. Not yours.

Some people might be thinking "I'll never trust him again. The trust has been broken and it will never be there again." Can you live with that? Can you love him without trust? Will that work for you? Some people can do this, and others can't.

You might also be thinking, "I should've seen it sooner, this should've happened sooner, I should've done something sooner". This is not your fault. Your partner is doing this program, it was not up to you to have found it sooner or pushed him towards it, or to help him to change sooner. Things are happening in the time that they're meant to be happening and the most important thing to acknowledge is that they are happening!

A CHANGE FOR THE BETTER

If he is attending the group, and you are hopeful of change in him, then this is not a time to start blaming yourself. Give him time to learn what he needs to do to change. If you don't see change, then get support for you.

You might be thinking, "He'll never be honest, he'll never make the change". Give him a chance. Start with small things.

Ask him some questions: "Did you like that movie?" Is he going to be honest to a simple question like that? If you're not sure if your partner is just saying what you want to hear you could ask him if he'd tell you if he didn't like it.

People are usually open about things such as asking if they liked their meal. Big lies can hurt, so start looking at the smaller statements.

Three actions you could take:

1. Ask questions about the present, don't focus on the past. The present is happening now, and we can't change the past, except in our mind or imagination. A question might be: What did you learn in the group today? Did you share in the group today? What was the topic of the group today? How was work?

2. Keep it simple. Something that you both know about or share a liking for. If you're looking for pleasant conversation, you might share something about your day. Don't ask about past relationships or negative situations that might bring up negative emotions about multiple layered issues. Keep it simple.

3. If you don't believe he's being honest, stay true to yourself and be honest. Focus on yourself being honest. If you don't believe him, tell him it's hard for you to believe him, so that it doesn't move into a relationship where trust is not present. Let him learn to be honest, if you can.

Activity: Try asking these questions in the 'here and now', not bringing up the past. Keep it simple and keep it about you and him. If you're not OK with the responses, let him know. Otherwise, tick that off as something that hopefully he has been honest about, and something that is a positive interaction in your communication together.

Try asking these questions after each group he attends. He may not always feel like talking about the group as he may be processing what he's heard or learned, but if he doesn't answer this week, he may answer during the week, or next week. Don't give up just yet, unless the violence or coercive control is still occurring. If it is, please call the women's advocate or someone you trust.

CHAPTER 4

THOUGHTS, FEELINGS AND BEHAVIOURS

Keep your thoughts positive because your thoughts become your words. Keep your words positive because your words become your behaviour. Keep your behaviour positive because your behaviour becomes your habits.
— *Mahatma Gandhi*

Psychologists are trained to work with peoples' thoughts, feelings and behaviours. It's important to understand the psychology behind the program that your partner is attending. Firstly, by doing so, you'll understand how he'll be learning what he's learning. He'll be engaging with others, listening to their thoughts and beliefs, hearing about their feelings, and trying to understand the female victims' feelings. They'll be seeing some of their behaviours and how they can use alternative, non-violent behaviours to manage the same situations in a non-violent way.

Understanding thoughts, feelings, and behaviours and how your partner will talk about them, should help you talk openly together. If you remember those three words - "thoughts, feelings, and behaviours" - they can guide your questions to your partner, for example "What are your thoughts about that?"; "How were you feeling when they said that?"; "How was the group behaving?" or "How did others in the group react to that?"

Beliefs

Domestic and family violence occurs when specific sets of beliefs are relearned during childhood and reinforced by parents, family, and society. Some of these beliefs relate to a man's position in the home, a man's superiority, a man's entitlement, a man's power, that a man is more important than a woman, that a man is stronger than a woman, that a man has the last word, or is in charge of decision-making.

The next two chapters will go further into beliefs, firstly yours and then his. Keep in mind, however, that the men's behaviour change programs are designed to challenge the beliefs that have resulted in violence against women, the women men supposedly love, the women who bear the man's children and nurture him as well as the children.

During the group programs, you may benefit from knowing what may be raised in conversations about his beliefs and how his beliefs may be challenged in the group program. There are likely to be beliefs that your partner has had that are going to be questioned. He's going to be thinking about whether his beliefs have helped him in his relationship with you, or not.

THOUGHTS, FEELINGS AND BEHAVIOURS

If your partner talks with you about something he's finding difficult to accept, you may be able to see that this is challenging his thoughts, feelings and behaviours. It may be easier for you to listen to him, and see his point of view, as well as hear the side that is being challenged, or the aspects that he's finding difficult to accept. Listen to him. He will talk, if you listen.

Give him some minimal encouragers, saying things like: "Yes"; "Oh"; "That's good"; or small words just to let him know you're listening. Also, keep talking, give him your opinion, give him some thoughts on what you believe, and then see if he gives you some minimal encouragers back. Then you'll know if he's listening to you.

Men who attend behaviour change programs can be successful in abstaining from domestic and family violence, and controlling behaviours. The success stories are really good. When we hear the positive comments that men make at the end of the program when they've come to understand the concepts being taught, they're so grateful, and so positive about moving forward in their lives without violence or threatening behaviour.

If men aren't getting it, if their beliefs are too strong to change, and are supported by all men around them in their lives, if they don't accept some of the concepts that come up in the program, they'll usually leave the group program. They'll make a decision that it isn't a good fit for them. This is likely to mean that their desire for power and control is more important than the others around them. They won't stay, so you'll know, unless there's something else going on.

If he leaves the group

If your partner leaves half-way through the group program, ask him about it, because there could be a number of other reasons he's unable to continue. There could be a clash of personalities, or a clash with another man, or other men, in the group. This typically doesn't happen because the facilitators have usually screened the applicants in a detailed manner and allocated them to a group that should ideally be OK with them. But it may happen. If a man does not feel safe in the group, he may need to leave. If the information doesn't resonate with him, he may feel that he's wasting his time, or just not ready to make the change. If you're comfortable doing so, you could suggest that he talks with one of the co-facilitators.

If he has been court-ordered to attend the group, he may need a reminder that he's been court-ordered and that the group is important for him and that it's vitally important for him to contact a co-facilitator between groups, before the next group, to discuss the situation he's in, and to see if the co-facilitator can encourage him to continue to attend the group, or find an alternative option for him. He may be surprised at the support he receives.

But, it is not your responsibility to ensure that your partner continues to attend the group. It should be his decision, it's his commitment, and you can delegate that task to the co-facilitators. You're not responsible for his completion of the program. You can encourage it, but you're not responsible – he is. It's an important message in the group that men take responsibility for their thoughts, feelings and behaviours, even when it may feel like it's someone else's fault that he's uncomfortable in the group.

Your partner is going to learn to be accountable for his actions, rather than blaming others. He's going to learn to identify his beliefs and look at his previous 'blaming' behaviour. Some of the statements he may have said in the past such as: "It's all her fault"; "She made me do it!"; "It's her family"; "It's the children"; "I did nothing wrong"; "I'm just tired, I work hard all day, so don't push me" should become statements of the past. He's going to start looking at some of those statements right from the very first session.

You could ask your partner: "What are you learning in the group in relation to violence?"; "How does this relate to us?" That should get him thinking. He'll learn about non-violent and non-threatening behaviour. He'll learn by other men talking about their relationships, and their actions, by responding on his own, about his own views, or by working in a small group. He'll also learn from watching brief videos of other couples interacting.

Let's look at the three characters we've been reading about and how they responded after the first group session.

Scenario 1

After the first group session for Nate, he decided that he was going to stop calling Natalia names and try to stop swearing at her. At his second group session he reported that he had not called Natalia names but slipped up a few times with his swearing.

Scenario 2

After the first few group sessions, Jackson hadn't changed his actions towards Olivia. He was so sure she loved him despite what he did or said to her. He was committed to no violence and he didn't hit, push, shove, or hurt her in any way, but he showed coercive control and the same attitude towards her that he'd always had.

Scenario 3

Chris reported that he wasn't seeing much of Emily, so he didn't have time to be controlling or violent towards her. Chris was out a lot, and it became clear, later on, that he was out with Taylor, so his abuse towards Emily was silent, and related to his dishonesty, lack of respect, self-focus, and lack of empathy and appreciation. In Emily's case she wasn't physically abused, she was emotionally abused, and Chris wasn't reporting that to the group until it was too late, and Emily had been hurt and felt betrayed.

In these cases, behaviours or actions may be what your partner says or doesn't say, what he does or doesn't do, and how he treats you or doesn't treat you.

You may have some objections such as "I don't want to know what's in the program, I just want him fixed". But, if he's the only one that knows, it won't be so equal. If he's the only one that has knowledge of the program, it'll be hard to for you to pull him up for doing things he shouldn't be doing. It's part of being equal, that you both have an understanding of what's occurring in the program. If he's the only one that knows what's going on, it's not equal. Knowledge is power, and if you don't have the knowledge, only he does, he may still be in a position of power, and your relationship could quickly slide back into old patterns of behaviour that brought you both to this situation in the first place.

You might think "I don't care what he learns". But, it's healthy to talk about what each other is doing. If he talks about what he's doing, and sees you're listening, then hopefully you can talk about what you are doing and he'll listen to you, and you both have debriefing time at the end of your day. Some people who are busy with work and parenting may catch up once a week and talk about their week, but for others it may be a daily occurrence. To help re-enforce memories of what's occurred in the men's behaviour change group, it'd be ideal to talk with your partner after the group, or even the next day if he's still processing what he's learned.

You may be thinking "I don't want to hear about the other men in the group". If your partner is talking about another person in the group, be aware that the men are encouraged not to disclose confidential information outside the group, but he might say something at some stage. If you don't want to hear it, let him know. It's important for you to know how he is learning, and he will be learning from listening to others in the group. If he tells you about something said in the group, then he's re-enforcing it in his own mind and in his memory. It may be OK if he talks about others' behaviours in the group without mentioning names, as long as you're comfortable to hear it.

For example, if your partner said something like: "I was telling my story and someone interrupted me and then they reacted negatively and it wasn't OK". It's important that he talks with you about his behaviour, because he's learning that it's not nice to be interrupted, or it's not nice for someone to be negative towards you. How many times has he done this to you? This could be related to the feelings he may have had in his relationship with you. He may be starting to see the reactions and responses from others in the group. He may be starting to reflect on his past behaviour in relation to times that he may have done this to you.

Your communication between groups may be about him learning from his interactions with other men, or their reactions with their partners, and then generalising it to his own previous behaviour.

When your partner returns from attending his group you could:

1. Ask your partner about his experience in the group. As he talks, you may ask: "When they talked about this how did it make you feel?"
"What was going through your mind; what were your thoughts at that time?"
"How does this affect the way you believe people should behave in a relationship?"

2. Ask him what he learned. Ask if he watched a video, and what it was about. Ask if he shared information in the group. Did he do written work or small group work? Ask him to read you what he wrote. Show an interest.

3. Then, tell him what you did while he was at the group, if you're comfortable telling him. This way, you're both getting a chance to talk about what you've done, and this is positive communication, taking turns to share information, and listen to each other, as equals.
If your partner doesn't ask you what you did, try to tell him: "Now I'm going to tell you what I did while you were at the group…". Hopefully he'll listen. If not, remind him that you've just listened to him and it'd be nice if he listened to you.

The groups can be a positive way for you both to re-engage in pleasant communication activities. Remember that if this doesn't go well for you, you can call the women's advocate to discuss it further. She may be able to give you more tips on this process, given your specific situation.

CHAPTER 5

WHAT DO YOU BELIEVE?

To start off we need to have a look at the question, "What is a belief?" A belief is something that you see as being true. It may exist or it may be something that you find exists. A belief may be "I'm a good person". A belief might be "Good people do good things and don't do bad things".

In this chapter we want to get an understanding of beliefs, and the difference between things that you may believe and what your partner may believe, and see if there's a difference. We also want to check for irrational beliefs, beliefs that aren't based on reality. Sometimes we can develop beliefs that aren't exactly correct, that are not based on evidence, and we might need to challenge those beliefs. With our beliefs we also need to be honest with ourselves. One of the things that comes up when talking about domestic and family violence is that people stay in relationships when there is domestic and family violence. If the male person using coercive control is trying to be entitled, important and being in control of

A CHANGE FOR THE BETTER

everyone in the household, he may have a belief that this is his role as a male person in the house.

We can see and experience physical and verbal abuse quite clearly, and these behaviours may be why your partner has been charged and why he's attending the men's behaviour change group. When the behaviours listed below occur, it's pretty clear it's domestic and family violence:

Slapping	
Hitting	
Shoving	
Scratching	
Biting	
Pinning	
Blocking	
Hair pulling	
Squeezing you	
Grabbing your arms, legs, body, hair	
Grabbing or hitting your breasts, belly, buttocks, vagina	
Placing his hands around your neck, holding or pinning you by the neck	
Hurting your pets, as a way to hurt you	
Forcing you to touch him in ways you don't like	
Touching you in ways you don't like	
Forcing you to have sex	
Rape	
Pressuring you to have sex or for specific sexual acts	

WHAT DO YOU BELIEVE?

Making demeaning or sexual comments on front of others	
Calling you names in front of others	
Swearing at you, when alone or in front of others	
Using a weapon (knife, gun, bat, cane, stick, or other object) to threaten or hurt you	
Pretending to hit you so you flinch, then laughing at or ridiculing you	
Hurting you in other ways	

We also look at a level of control in the house where the woman may not be feeling safe, or the woman suffers from physical violence or threatened behaviour, then people wonder why women stay in the relationship. This can be related back to what people believe.

When people get married or move in together these actions can involve strong beliefs such as "When we get married it's for life" or "When we live together it's the same as being married because we're de facto, and therefore it's for life". When we have children we may believe "We must stay with their father" or "We must have a father figure in the house for the children". We may have a belief that "It was our fault that he was violent, not his fault", especially if your partner has been telling you it's your fault. We may come to believe that.

The old saying, "If we're going to keep doing what we've always done, we're going to keep getting what we've always had" is relevant here. It relates to staying stuck and not making changes. When looking at your partner making some change, we want to be able to understand what might be keeping him stuck in terms of making change. We can bring this back to the beliefs that people have, including your beliefs.

A CHANGE FOR THE BETTER

The same applies for you – if your beliefs stay the same your life won't change. If you believe your partner won't change it's probably going to make it difficult to try to put some of his changes into practice.

When we're looking at relationships, we look at "What is love?" and our beliefs around love. We look at "What is non-violent behaviour?" and "What do you believe is appropriate behaviour, and what should occur in a loving and intimate relationship?"

"What is violence?" We talk about coercive control being a lead up to physical and threatening or sexual violence. An impact of imposing oneself onto another person with the intention of controlling them or causing harm. We do explore what is coercive control. The laws have recently changed in Australia in terms of coercive control being a criminal offence.

If you're staying in a relationship where there is ongoing physical violence you could start looking at your beliefs around that. A man could have a belief "I'm doing this because I love you"; "I'm in charge of the household and I'm taking control because this is love". But is it actually your definition of what love is meant to be in a relationship?

Men have been known to tell their female partners, "You'll never find another man who loves you this much" and that might be his belief, but is it actually your belief? Do you come to believe that you won't find another man who loves you? Is this the first man you've been in a relationship with? If it isn't, you have found another man who loves you, and if you're not in this relationship you could find another man again. People continue to experience relationships well into their 80s and 90s. Some elderly people do find love again. Their spouse or partner might have died or they've separated and they find love later in life.

WHAT DO YOU BELIEVE?

Men can sometimes have the belief "I'll die without you" or "You'll die without me" or "I can't leave my kids" but these things don't necessarily happen. He won't die without you (unless he's having suicidal thoughts) and you won't die without him, and people do have subsequent relationships.

You might be saying "I'm with him because I love him", but if there's control and violence, is that really love? Look back to the time when you first met each other and you were blissfully in love or infatuated and you both thought about each other all the time, you had loving thoughts of each other and had lovely experiences together.

You might have a thought "I forgive him". Does he deserve forgiveness? Is what he has done to you something that you can forgive? For some people it will be, some people are good at forgiving, while others don't like to forgive certain things. But if you're going to continue in your relationship, an element of forgiveness would be a good thing. If you can't forgive, then accepting and moving on is another means of working with progressing your relationship. When we can't forgive, or accept and move on, then we might continue to maintain negative communication styles with our partner.

If you had a belief "He was helping me by taking control", it's important to know that when one person is in control of a relationship and the other person has limited control, statistically we have seen that eventually that can lead to violence, especially when the person not in control decides they'd like to have some control, and the person in control doesn't agree or let go of their control. Violence is one way to show their control.

A CHANGE FOR THE BETTER

Activity

1. Make a list of ten actions that you believe represent what love is.

2. Write down ten loving sentences a person might say to someone they love.

3. Write down ten actions that are not based on love.

4. Look at the difference between the items in these three different lists.

Here is a list of behaviours classified as coercive control. Tick any that you've experienced, or make a mental note of them.

Table 1. (Adapted from Lundy & Patrissi, 2011)

Calling you names ("Bitch", "slut", "whore", "psycho")	
Belittling your dreams or goals for your future	
Putting you down about you weight, your body, your looks ("you're fat", "you're ugly")	
Keeping you from seeing your friends or family	
Ruining your relationships with friends and family	
Telling you where you can and can't go	
Telling you what you can and can't buy	
Telling you what you can and can't wear (this does not include when you ask him for advice on what to wear if you can't decide)	
Giving you only a small allowance (money)	
Not allowing you access to the money in your joint bank account	

WHAT DO YOU BELIEVE?

Ignoring you to punish you	
Demanding constant attention from you	
Demanding that you make or bring him food or drinks	
Blocking your way	
Laughing at you when your creation or behaviour is not funny	
Telling you "it's all in your head"	
Calling you "crazy" or "mentally ill", making you feel crazy	
Scaring you	
Threatening to hurt or take your children	
Threatening to hurt your family or friends	
Threatening to hurt your pets	
Lying to you	
Having an affair	
Accusing you of having an affair	
Telling you that you can't talk about a certain topic, or reacting badly if you bring up a certain topic	
Blaming you for something he did	
Punishing you for standing up to him	
Making you feel more controlled than valued in the relationship	
Asking if you're afraid of him	
Not taking responsibility for his own actions	
Give and take in the relationship is not equal	
Doing less chores around the house than you do	
Doing any of these on an ongoing basis e.g. more than once, after you've asked him to stop doing it, or he's agreed to stop doing it	

Can you see any of your ten actions that represent love?
Can you see any of your ten loving sentences?
Can you see actions that are not based on love?

When a couple experiences domestic and family violence we can look back at their relationship history and we can usually identify elements of coercive control in the lead up to verbal, physical, and/or sexual violence.

The bigger picture

Evan Stark, researcher, forensic social worker, sociologist, and author of 'Coercive Control: How Men Entrap Women in Personal Life' suggests that men can use coercive control to extend their dominance over a period of time in ways that reduce women's autonomy, isolates them, and affects the most intimate aspects of their lives. He analyses the cases of three women who were tried for domestic crimes, and he shows that their reactions can be better understood under a framework of being victims of coercive control rather than as "battered wives".

He explains that most abused women who seek help have done so after their rights and liberties have been compromised, not because they have been physically assaulted. Stark developed a coercive control model that focuses on three aspects of abuse: why these relationships endure, why abused women develop a profile of problems seen among no other group of assault victims, and why the legal system has failed to bring justice for them, taking coercive control to a platform of being a human rights violation which affects women's freedom in their everyday lives.

To this end, we must never lose focus of domestic and family violence, nor minimise coercive control as part of the domestic violence cycle.

CHAPTER 6
WHAT DID HE BELIEVE?

Beginning in childhood, people develop certain ideas about themselves, other people, and their world.
— *Judith Beck*

The person regards these ideas as absolute truths – just the way things "are".
— *Aaron Beck*

In this chapter we have a look at some typical male beliefs that may have led him to engage in domestic and violence. When we look at these, we see that these are some of the beliefs that the men's behaviour change programs are trying to challenge, with men, so that other men can learn from reflecting back on some of the beliefs that may not have been rational or respectful.

A CHANGE FOR THE BETTER

When we look at a belief it needs to be based on reality, something for which we can find evidence. We're going to try to get any idea of how he has been thinking, try to understand his beliefs and further identify those which may be behind thoughts and feelings and behaviours that lead to coercive control. We want to acknowledge that all men are not the same. Not all men feel entitled and want to control or want to exert power over other people. Not all men believe that they are the head of the household and that what they say goes, and everyone must listen to them. There are men who are keenly interested in their partners' choices, their partners' thoughts and dreams, their partners' wishes, and their partners' well-being 100% of the time. We also want to get a baseline of where he's at now, so that you can tell when he changes.

The statistics for emotional abuse, according to the Personal Safety Survey from the Australian Bureau of Statistics, released in August 2022, stated that an estimated 2.2 million adult women (23 per cent) and 1.4 million adult men (16 per cent) have experienced emotional abuse by a partner at some point since the age of 15.

In the Personal Safety Survey, it is stated that *"partner emotional abuse occurs when a person is subjected to behaviours that are aimed at preventing or controlling their behaviour, causing them emotional harm or fear. These behaviours are characterised in nature by their intent to manipulate, control, isolate or intimidate the person they are aimed at. They are generally repeated behaviours and include psychological, social, financial and verbal abuse"* (https://www.abs.gov.au/media-centre/media-releases/36-million-people-experienced-partner-emotional-abuse).

A contrast here is that if he doesn't think and believe this way, what else could be going on? If it's not thoughts of entitlement, and power and control, thinking that he must be in charge and

WHAT DID HE BELIEVE?

men are superior, then why has he ended up engaging in domestic violence?

What are we looking at with domestic and family violence and coercive control? We're looking at power, we're looking at the one person in the household that can make the decisions, who sees themselves as being in charge of the money or the purchase of the house, or moving out of the house or where the children go to school. If you disagree, he will still get his way. We look at control, being able to control people, where everyone in the house has to do what he wants because if they don't, he won't be happy. This is a belief that he has to be happy and is not considering whether or not everyone else in the house is happy. They have to try to be happy when he's happy, try to be content when he's content, and amenable to his decisions.

There's a sense of entitlement as a male person. He feels able to take this power and control, a sense that he is right, that a female can have an opinion but his opinion is always right and superior, and everyone must accede to his opinion. His belief is that the man is the head of the household so therefore he has the decisions to make. If others can't make a decision or don't agree it's bad luck, because he is in charge, confirming the belief that the man is superior, the man makes all the decisions.

The entitled man doesn't have to consult anyone. He can go out and buy himself a new car. He doesn't ask "Should we spend this much money?" or "Is there something else we should buy?" or "Is it going to be suitable for the children?" or "If we have another baby, will there be room in the car?" or "Will I consider certain aspects and get an opinion from someone else in the household?" Basically, the entitled man believes he can do whatever he likes. If he chooses to go out drinking before he goes home he can do that. He doesn't need permission or to tell anyone what he's doing.

When considering what coercive control is, we can look back at beliefs, thoughts, intentions, and situations that are controlling from the entitled male person to others in the household. We look at physical violence, any exertion of force upon another person, and we look at sexual violence. This is any act of sex without consent, even if it is rolling over in the middle of the night, hugging and kissing and engaging in sex when, as far as he knows, you were asleep. Whether you appear to wake up or not, we must look at consent, just as we would if a new acquaintance is too drunk to provide consent.

On the other hand, we can look at a violent sexual assault, when the man may have the belief that he's entitled to have sex whenever he wants because he believes his wife is his possession, and he can take her body for his own sexual pleasure whenever he chooses to do so. That is sexual violence.

If you are doubting the success of these programs for men's behaviour change, if you believe he can't change, consider this. What if he is someone that it is so embedded in his belief system that he can't change his behaviour? If your partner can't change then you are going to have some decisions to make. You're an adult and you're able to make decisions. Women who aren't supported to make these very serious decisions can end up being very seriously injured or even killed if they stay in abusive relationships. Women who have support to end a relationship have a better chance of leaving without harm coming to them or to their children.

"What if I change my mind?" you might ask. What if you've stayed in the relationship so your partner can get through this program

WHAT DID HE BELIEVE?

and then, part-way through, you find you're not trusting him, you find you're not even respecting him, you're feeling unsafe, you're feeling uncomfortable, your mood is always low and you're not happy in the marriage or the relationship. These might be reasons why you might change your mind. The old saying, "It's a woman's prerogative to change her mind" is very appropriate here. You should have the ability, choice, space, and freedom to change your mind, if you choose to do so. It is within the realm of possibility for all women, just as it is for men.

It is important to note that if you change your mind and you don't want to be living with your partner, it is a time that can be dangerous for women as we find that a lot of domestic violence occurs when women attempt to leave the relationship. So I would strongly encourage you to seek as much support as possible before you tell him you're leaving. Make doubly sure you have processes in place, support for yourself and your children, and that you don't do it alone. Ensure that several people are informed of what you're doing, when you're doing it, and where you will be and where he will be so that any sort of separation or break or end of relationship is done very safely and securely.

Of course, this could also be just a break. You could ask your partner to give you some time because you're not recovering as well emotionally as you'd hoped from any domestic violence and that while he completes the men's behaviour change program he'll be supported because he'll have the group and the facilitators in the program, and whatever other supports he may have such as family, psychologists, support workers, his GP, or another men's group, men's shed, sporting club, or work colleagues. He's likely to have that support and if you did have a break, he could continue to work on himself to a point where you can both keep in contact and rebuild your trust, and maybe reconsider the options for your relationship.

A CHANGE FOR THE BETTER

Or, it may just be that you've tried and that's it, you have had enough, it is over, you don't want a break, and you don't ever want to be going back, and that's OK. You would need support and should try to be tactful and respectful in your delivery of information about your decision about the relationship or the marriage.

Another thought might be: What if he becomes someone I don't respect because he doesn't have that bravado, male strength, and bad-boy attitude, and I decide I don't like him if he's not masculine? Well, what if that means that you're telling me you don't want respect? Because the bad boys are the men that typically don't respect women, use coercive control, and physical and sexual violence. It might seem tough, but it's not ok. It injures women, it hurts women emotionally and it is not an equal relationship. It is leaving the potential for ongoing coercive control and physical and/or sexual violence.

Three things that you might do:

1. Decide what you'll do if he doesn't change.
   Have an idea of what you'll do if he's violent again. Will you wait until he's finished the program? Will you tell him straight away? Will you try to roll with it? These are all decisions that you can consider and make, and it would be good to try to make a decision so that you know where things are going for yourself, as well as for him. Your life has some element of predictability, because sometimes domestic and family violence is just unpredictable, but sometimes it's very predictable. Some women can pick up on it every easily, for example, if he's had a few drinks he's going to get irritable, if he's had an argument with his parents, friends, or colleagues he might get irritable. You, having lived with him, are likely to know better than

anyone else, what may trigger him. For some men, it can be difficult to anticipate when he may be triggered.

2. Know your options.
   If your partner is someone you want to stay with, you know his behaviour, if he's already done a men's behaviour change program, he may have already done the Betterment Program, and the violent behaviour starts again. There are Level 2 behaviour change programs that he can attend. You can "plant the seed" that you're aware that there's a Level 2 behaviour change program that takes things further than the first program he attended. Maybe together you could both talk about a decision for him to do a "next level" program. Make a call to the facilitators of the Betterment Program and ask about Level 2 programs.

3. Look for signs of change.
   How is he changing now? Even the little things: giving you a kiss goodbye before he goes to work, bringing something home for you or for the children; doing acts of kindness for you and compare them with last year. Was he doing this last year, or prior to starting the MBCP? Let this be a comparison to see small aspects of change. Is he smiling at you more? Is he giving you more compliments? Is he coming and helping you with the children or with the chores? Try to identify these behaviours, try to really see them. If he's never done these things before and he starts doing them, they are signs that he is trying to make changes in his thinking and beliefs. He may previously have believed that he could do whatever he liked, that you'd never leave him, and he may now be seeing the need to work on your relationship and be nice to you so you won't leave him. He needs to include you in decision-making and say some of

the things and do some of those actions that he did when you first met each other and fell in love, or that may be on your list of loving statements and actions.

*Despite how angry, hurt, insecure, or unhappy your partner may appear to be, his abusive behaviour is rooted far more in how he **thinks** than in how he **feels**.*
*The answer to what has gone wrong lies primarily not in his **heart** - except for his lack of compassion towards you - but rather in his **mind**.*
— Bancroft and Patrissi (2011)

CHAPTER 7

WHERE'S THE RESPECT?

Change in all things is sweet.
— *Aristotle*

Respect is one of the greatest expressions of love.
— *Miguel Angel Ruiz*

When you're speaking of being given respect, what is it you're asking for? How do we know what respect is, and how do you know when you get it? Basically, we look at respect as being allowed to have choices. Being respected means being true to yourself, not changing your mind, and not settling for less. Not changing your goals when you get what you want.

What does respect look like? You know what lack of respect looks like; it looks like coercive control, someone being in power and control, entitlement and authority, and an inability to have a say or contribute to a decision.

Examples of respect are:

Someone acknowledging you
Someone being grateful for what you do
Someone listening to you and not responding with negativity
Someone understanding your choices in relation to marriage or relationship
Someone accepting and respecting your friends and your hobbies
Talking about parenting together
Someone taking your parenting choices on board and discussing them
Respecting your desire to have a job
Respecting your religion or spirituality
Acknowledging and understanding who you are

In the MBCP we require men to respect their partner. If the male participants are saying things like "She did this, she said that" we ask them what your first name is and we ask them to use your name, which is respectful to you. You are not "the missus" or "the old lady" or "she".

Respect is also really appreciating who you are and the contributions that you make to the relationship or to the family, as well as who your friends are and the contributions they make to your happiness and well-being.

During the program we like to emphasise that when men show their respect to women they want their female partner to have positive thoughts and positive feelings. They want her to be able to have a job as well as have a home. They want her to have a good relationship with no DFV. They share any problems that you may have. They give respect and they get respect in return. If your partner is giving you respect they usually feel good as they feel like a good person and are acknowledging you as a good person too.

Overall, you feel better, they feel better, and life is good. You're able to be you because aspects of you are respected and you're able to allow them to be themselves as the respect is reciprocated.

So what is lack of respect? What does that look like?

It includes:
Name calling
Calling you something other than your name
Refusing to listen to your opinion
Not taking the time to try to understand your opinion or position
Refusing to acknowledge your opinion
Disregarding your parenting style
Behaviour which usually leads to a disagreement.

What does it look like when you respect your partner? Do you listen to, acknowledge and understand who he is as a person (the positive aspects)?

Going back to when you first began your relationship, what was the respect like then? For example, your partner may have told you what he really likes about you, as he tried to forge the relationship. You might have been working in a full-time job and he might've said he really respects that fact that you're working so hard. There is a time when you're both trying to have a relationship and making a commitment together and you're using nice sentences with each other, saying nice things, and feeling respect for each other.

A CHANGE FOR THE BETTER

You might tell yourself that you don't need respect. Well, you do. If there's no respect, it's not an equal relationship. It's highly likely that your partner wants respect and if he wants respect and you're thinking that you don't need it, then it's not equal. He retains power and control in the relationship, which could result in abuse and eventually violence.

You might say to yourself "I get a little respect" or "I get respect from his parents". That's not enough. It needs to come from him and it needs to be decent respect, not just a little every now and then. It must be always.

Let's now head back to the three scenarios we looked at in previous chapters, and consider how these men may or may not have demonstrated respect towards their partners.

Scenario 1

Nate realised very early in the program that he had not respected Natalia. He realised that he called her names, blamed her for his bad mood, didn't listen to her, didn't ask her what she'd like or what she thought. He identified early that when he loves someone, he should give them compliments, words of affirmation, and whisper sweet sentences in their ear, including promises of change when abuse or violence has previously occurred. How else can trust be rebuilt honestly and effectively?

Scenario 2

When Jackson spoke of Olivia, he was so sure she would agree to all of his desires and goals. He was sure she would never leave him and that she agreed, somehow, that he was the most important person in the house. This belief reflected his sense of entitlement and power. Where did this leave her? Where was the respect for her or where was her existence?

Olivia said that Jackson talked with her about his experiences in the group. He talked about his thoughts, his feelings, his reactions to the other men. She soon realised that Jackson didn't ask her how she felt about his progress, how she felt about their relationship, whether she thought he had changed or was learning anything that may benefit her. He was doing the program not for her, but for him. He didn't even ask her what she did while he was at the group. Whilst he should have been working in the program for himself and addressing his thoughts, feelings, behaviours and beliefs, life included Olivia. A relationship involves two people.

Olivia took her concerns to the women's advocate and talked through her thoughts and feelings about the relationship and how it was progressing after the serious violence that had occurred. She wasn't happy, she wasn't seeing Jackson trying to re-establish trust, and she didn't feel any better than the day after he assaulted her. And she believed that he hadn't even noticed that she wasn't happy. She was starting to think about leaving the relationship and she began exploring her options.

The women's advocate stepped up her interest in Olivia because the statistics show that when women leave a relationship they're at a high risk of violence from their partner. She started booking appointments with Olivia on a weekly basis and checked in with her by phone almost daily. They revisited the safety plan together and added additional support people and safety strategies to the plan. The women's advocate alerted other support services listed in the safety plan that Olivia may be thinking about leaving the relationship.

Scenario 3

For Chris, we see a classic self-focused man, who is disrespecting women frequently. Chris' ex-partner had left him due to a serious assault for which he was imprisoned. He talked to an ex-partner of a male friend to engage with her while he was in jail, which in some cases breaches the 'men's code' of engaging with a friend's ex-partner. Of course, not all men adhere to such a code. Emily visited him in jail, at a cost to herself for transport to get to the jail, which was some distance from her home. She deposited money into his jail account, provided her address for his release, and assisted him to obtain work only to find him engaging with another woman, Taylor, within a week of his release from jail.

The lack of respect for Emily is clear, as she was unlikely to have been aware that Chris engaged with another partner shortly after his release from jail. His lack of honesty to both of these women was disrespectful.

Three things for you to think about:

1. Think of someone that you respect, other than your partner. Picture that person in your mind. It may be a parent, an aunt or uncle, a work colleague, or a friend. What do you respect about them?

2. How do you show them respect? How do you let them know that you respect them?

3. How do they treat you? How do they respect you?

WHERE'S THE RESPECT?

See Table 1. For simple signs of respect, and warning signs that a partner may not respect you (from Bancroft and Patrissi, 2011)

Table 1.

Signs of respect	Warning signs for lack of respect
He's a good listener	He has high levels of self-involvement and self-centredness
He's respectful of you	He makes lots of excuses and/or promises
He has long-lasting relationships with others	He has to have his own way
He can manage his own life	He shows jealousy and possessiveness
He practices what he preaches	He always has to drink or use drugs
He's respectful of his former partners	People are trying to warn you about him
He can look after himself	He pressures you
He makes your wishes a priority	He's secretive

CHAPTER 8
CAN IT REALLY GET BETTER?

There is a sub-group of chronically violent men who are largely unresponsive to these programs.
— *Edward Gondolf*

The Betterment Domestic and Family Violence Intervention Program at Akers Psychology tries to achieve a change to make life better for relationships, better for families, better for society, and especially better for you. So, if you're still in the relationship, your partner is attending the group, you're giving it a last chance for him to make a change, but the change he's been promising for quite some time hasn't really happened yet, you may be wondering if it can really get better,.

If this is the case, it is vitally important to act now if your partner is still being violent towards you, while he is in the group program. If, despite him signing a contract committing to non-violence, he is

A CHANGE FOR THE BETTER

clearly not changing, it's not a good sign. Some men don't change. In this case you must either make a decision about the relationship or talk with a friend, family, or women's advocate, or get a support person and talk directly with the police. Do not put up with violence, abuse, or coercive control while waiting to see change.

If your partner is on a court order, a domestic violence order, or if he's on parole, probation, or a good behaviour bond, and he engages in further domestic and family violence, then the judicial system is going to be a consequence for him.

Be aware of the supports available for you.

Here's a list of supports for people living in Australia:
The women's advocate of the group program your partner is attending
1800 Respect: 1800 737 732
Sexual Assault Helpline Call: 1800 010 120
Full Stop Sexual and Domestic and Family Violence Helpline: 1800 385 578
Full Stop Rainbow Sexual and Domestic and Family Violence Helpline: 1800 497 212
Domestic and family violence prevention centres in your state or territory
Lifeline: 131114
Kids Helpline: 1800 551 800
Your counsellor or psychologist
The court: Domestic Violence Order
Department of Child Safety in your area
The Police, call 000 if you are not safe. Police stations have a Domestic Violence Officer whom you can meet with to talk through any violence occurring.

If this is not the case, and your partner is trying to change, if you are not experiencing violence, abuse or coercive control, then we can look at the second instance, and that is trying to trust the process.

If you've been trusting your partner and initially things were OK, but now you're thinking that it hasn't quite worked, bring it back to the process. Learn to challenge some of his pre-existing beliefs, trusting yourself that you've made a good decision to give him another chance. To give him a chance to make a change for the better, trusting your partner with baby-steps or small increments, trying to trust that he can learn something and make some changes,

Try to trust the extended support that's being offered in the program, from the women's advocate to the other staff or co-facilitators, or even some of the other men, that they are working with your partner and helping him to make change. You may happen to know one or more of the partners of the men in the program or even some of your supports, your parents or your female or male friends. Trust the system, society, the criminal justice system. This is a community approach and the community is there to support you. You can reach out to them if you are not safe or OK.

Relapse facts

There have been evaluations of men's behaviour change programs at the two years post group attendance mark, but, according to long-time researcher of men's behaviour change programs, Edward Gondolf, there is a subgroup of chronically violent men who do not respond to these programs and give these programs a bad name. The good news is that the vast majority of male attendees show a reduction in abuse over time, and the longer the group program, the better the success of the program. If your partner has attended a shorter anger management or behaviour change program and you haven't seen much change, he may require a longer program over a period of 20-25 weeks or more.

In some areas of the United States, programs run for 12 months, as their beliefs and behaviours that have been role-modelled since early childhood and re-enforced in society can be quite entrenched. Men's behaviour change programs embedded in a community-controlled response to domestic and family violence provide a better success rate than programs in a stand-alone setting. These programs provide consequences for relapses (through the court), monitoring of behaviour (by probation and parole), support for the victims (women's advocate), in conjunction with the men's behaviour change programs. If men relapse there are consequences, and change takes time.

Talking about change

When we talk about change, and we've noted that change may not happen straight away, it's good to acknowledge the Stages of Change Model and look at where your partner is at right now. Prochaska and Di Clemente developed the Stages of Change Model to help explain why change doesn't happen overnight for all people.

How will you know if he's making change? How will you know if he's working towards it? Where will you be? What will be happening for you? For your children? How will you feel about change in your relationship? Will you trust it? Change can be very hard but if we accept support or assistance from others, to see things differently from the way we've seen them before, we may find it easier to accept.

CAN IT REALLY GET BETTER?

When looking at the Stages of Change Model in Table 1, the first stage of change is Pre-Contemplation. Contemplation means contemplating things, thinking about things. The Pre-Contemplation Stage of Change is where a person is not thinking about change. They're doing what they've been ordered, they're doing what everyone else wants them to do. They're coming along and doing what they think is expected but are not fully committed. He may be thinking, "Yes I can go along to a group but everything's fine, I'm fine, I'm still living in the house, I haven't been kicked out, I'm not in jail, I'm OK, that's it I don't need to do anything". That's Pre-Contemplation. Hopefully your partner is not necessarily in the Pre-Contemplation Stage and that should've been assessed prior to them being accepted into the program. It would have been assessed if he is engaging in the Betterment Program at Akers Psychology.

The first positive stage of change is just about thinking about change, and is called the Contemplation Stage of Change. This is where your partner is saying, "Hmm, maybe I do need to make some change. My parents have told me, my partner has told me, my doctor or my parole officer, or the magistrate or judge in the court has told me that I need to make some change...so many people have told me I need to make change, so maybe I do need to. Maybe this is where I need to go." It's only a slight change from Pre-Contemplation to Contemplation, but the fact that a person is thinking about making change means they're open to the idea of change and they're in a much better position to start to make some change. It all starts with our thought processes.

The next stage of change is the Decision Stage, which can also involve planning. This is when people are thinking about things, but haven't yet decided to make change, which is the next step. The earlier groups that your partner will be attending will get him thinking. The group sessions will be challenging his thoughts and beliefs. He'll be thinking, and thinking, and thinking, and hopefully he will get to the next stage of making a decision and start to engage in planning. Making a decision is about simply saying, "Yes, I'm going to do this". The planning at the decision stage is about when they might do it, and hopefully the answer is now, and then planning how are they going to do it. How are they going to do it? How are they going to trust the process of change? How are they going to feel about making that change and how is that going to change some of the beliefs they may have had since childhood or adolescence? Changes may go against the behaviour they've seen other men in their life perform.

Of course, this is only a decision. The next stage of change is the Action Stage and with action we need to see the person engaging in activity as a result of making the decision to make change. In this stage, hopefully you would start to see your partner listening to you, engaging you in the decision-making process, considering your feelings, asking how your day was, listening to you and maybe sharing some of his day with you. Ultimately, this should come back to having a discussion with you, and considering your thoughts, feelings and beliefs around your world and your relationship and maybe the parenting if you have children. The Action Stage is where you're going to start seeing some change happening in your partner and try to roll with the different feelings that may come up for him, or for you, and try to see where his action-taking ability is going to advance and improve your relationship.

It is acknowledged that at this stage, your partner may be wanting to take action, but you may not fully trust him yet. He may need to hear this, and you may have to tell him. It doesn't mean that if you don't trust him yet that he can't continue to make the change, and he should be encouraged to keep attending the group. He may find small things to be convenient excuses to cease his attendance at the group, but he needs to keep making the change, taking the action, and eventually some of that trust may come back for you. Now if it gets too hard, some life stressors occur, if he has any drug or alcohol issues that are complicating factors, if there is any other criminal activity or family issues, the next Stage of Change he reaches could be Relapse. At this stage it's so important that you have some safety to address any fall-out form a potential relapse. Just because relapse is on the Stage of Change Model doesn't mean that it will happen, but it suggests that we need to be prepared that it can happen.

It's good to look at the difference between what constitutes a lapse and a relapse. A lapse is one action, a relapse is ongoing actions of going back to old behaviours.

A lapse may occur when he has a bad day at work, came home and was angry, he shouted and he swore and it was something that he stated he would not do, and it's something that was not acceptable for you. He might have pulled himself up and said he won't do it again. If he follows through and doesn't do it again, then that's a lapse, it happened once. It's up to you and whether or not you accept that and depending on any ultimatum or agreement that you had together you might accept that and move on, as long as he doesn't lapse again, because if it happens more than once then it's a relapse and he has gone back to old behaviours. After that he may return to the Pre-Contemplation Stage, thinking "No this is me, I'm not changing, I've done nothing wrong". He may even think that he doesn't want to continue with the program, and stop going to his weekly groups.

Table 1. Stages of Change

Pre-Contemplation	Not contemplating or thinking about change, not seeing a need to change
Contemplation	Thinking about making change, considering options for change, but not acting on it yet
Decision/planning	Deciding to make a change; planning a date or time to start making change, but not acting on it yet
Action	Taking action! Starting to make the change, acting on the decision
Maintenance	Working on maintaining the changes made, and continuing to work on the changes made
Relapse	Falling back into old patterns or behaviours, e.g. violence, abuse, controlling behaviour

The Stages of Change Model shows that people can be in one stage of change or more than one stage of change at the same time, but it can go around and around in circles. At some point, the person needs to implement some long-term changes which would mean that as they're doing their action they move into a Maintenance Stage to prevent the relapse. The Maintenance Stage of Change is where they work on the change, they work on their promises that they've made to you and to themselves. They continue to work on the program, they continue to use the skills they've learned, they're taking responsibility for their behaviour, they're being accountable to you and to society, and they're using non-threatening behaviour in a very respectful manner, in terms of achieving some equality in the relationship with you.

CAN IT REALLY GET BETTER?

You may have some thoughts such as, "I know he'll change, he promised me he'll change, I know he'll be fine." But he might not. Sometimes we can be very trusting in relationships when we're promised things, but sometimes change can take time, and sometimes there are lapses. It is important that we all try to trust the process but we acknowledge that sometimes people can find change very difficult.

As discussed with the Stages of Change, it may take time. Check in on yourself and how you're feeling about your partner's progress. Ask him about how he's feeling, talk with your family and friends about what's been happening since he started the program, talk with the professionals, or the women's advocate, let her know what's happening.

Identify how the system is supporting you. Are you getting that extra support? Are people calling you and checking in to see if your partner is making change? Which Stage of Change are you at?

Hopefully you're not at the Pre-Contemplation Stage, because you're supporting your partner to make some change in the program. Maybe it's the Contemplation Stage where you're thinking about how things are going for him and for you, or maybe the Decision or Planning Stage if things are going well and you may be planning that weekend away, or a holiday, or something nice together. If you're at the Action Stage then you're actually doing that, you might book some accommodation or tell friends that you're coming to visit, or book a holiday together, whatever it may be. Then it's about maintenance. If you're away or doing something for work, maintain your stance, don't drop your guard, don't accept any abusive communication or actions and remember that just because you're not at home, doesn't mean that you shouldn't be treated respectfully.

A CHANGE FOR THE BETTER

What Stage of Change is your partner at? Have a think about where he's at. Is he at the Contemplation Stage? If he's attending the group program, he should be at the Action Stage, if he's booked in it's the decision-making stage with a bit of action included. If it's the early stages of the program for him he's at the Action Stage and he may be starting to enter the Maintenance Stage. Try to see where he's at. He may move through the program quickly, or he may move through it slowly, but either way, hopefully he's taking action.

There are three aspects of change that are important.

1. If you're having the thought, "He's not getting better" or "He's not showing any change", try to be patient. This is a 20-week program and in some cases it's 27 weeks. Try to trust yourself to be positive. Don't exceed your limits or give up too early. Change takes time. If he hasn't changed, check in with others, let him know. Have a talk about the fact that you may not feel there's a lot of change. Ask him if he thinks he's changing, ask him to tell you what he thinks he's doing that shows he's changing.

2. Some objections you may have might be, "Well he hasn't changed at all" but if he hasn't finished the program yet, give him some time. Running long-term programs, we find that some people do get quite involved in a program, but that shifting old beliefs can take repeated teaching to understand and grasp concepts, and that sometimes people don't grasp the concepts of programs until right at the end. He may have a lot of entrenched beliefs about power and control that require a lot of challenging. He may be clinging to control.

3. If you're thinking "I can't wait that long!" Ask yourself how long you've waited before. You've been with this person for quite some time. Would they wait for you? Maybe they would, maybe they wouldn't, but if you've been waiting for some time for them to get better, maybe you could wait a little longer while they're engaging in a structured opportunity to move towards change. This might feel like it's a lot to ask, given that they've been violent or abusive towards you, but it is a long program because change takes time. You can choose to end the relationship if you're not seeing results, but get a support person before you discuss your decisions with your partner, and take them with you when you tell him.

In the past when running counselling programs, some of the co-facilitators have come to me saying, "I don't think this particular person is getting it, they're not doing well, they're not grasping it". In these instances, I always respond in the same way. I'd say, "Give them some time, some people get it right towards the end".

You may be saying to yourself that you're scared to trust him. Again, just take small steps, and try to trust in the small steps. For example, if he offered to get you a cup of tea or coffee and you answered that you'd like that and he takes a little while to do it but eventually he does it, then that's trusting the process. Small steps to see that he's committed to doing something and does actually achieve it.

Three actions to take at the end of this chapter are:

1. Decide what trust is. What does a person have to do for you to trust them?

A CHANGE FOR THE BETTER

2. Decide what you think trust is for him. What does he expect in terms of trust?

3. Identify the differences between the two and attempt to bring the two closer together. If you want him to trust you more, can you trust him more? In a relationship where you're sharing a lot of emotional and physical intimacy it is usually with a person that you trust more than anyone in the world, maybe more than your parents, but trying to trust each other at a different level can really help couples move forward.

CHAPTER 9

CHILDREN MATTER

---◇◇---—o—---◇◇---

Your children are aware of the abuse. Children's interpretations can matter as much as their experiences. Your children are frightened.
Children believe they are to blame. Your children want to talk about the abuse but they feel that they can't.
— *Bancroft (2004)*

During the Betterment Program or another domestic and family violence intervention program that your partner may be attending, he will be required to discuss the effect that domestic and family violence may have had on you and others. Typically this means the children, the other family members, but may include family friends, neighbours, or members of the public. Your partner is going to be asked to take responsibility for the effect his behaviour has had on others, to acknowledge others have been affected, and to acknowledge the harm. He will be asked to

A CHANGE FOR THE BETTER

focus on someone else other than himself, and to start to practice empathy: the act of putting himself in the other person's shoes and trying to imagine what that might have been like for them.

The other thing that your partner will be focusing on during this program is how they can be a better father to the children. Some of the things he'll be encouraged to look at are: spending time with the children; sharing the parenting; sharing the responsibility of being a parent with you/not just expecting you to do everything; or expecting that you're doing the domestic aspects of the parenting, for example: making school lunches; getting them breakfast; doing the bathing; getting them to bed. He'll be encouraged to co-parent and share the jobs that are not described as a gender role. Many young children have stated that their favourite memories have been Mum bathing them and getting them ready for bed and Dad cleaning their teeth and reading them a bedtime story. The shared care and shared parenting is often extremely memorable for children.

Other children have talked about their parents doing alternate nights: one night Mum reads their bedtime story, and the next night Dad would do it, or one night Mum would supervise bath-time, cleaning teeth and bedtime story and the next night Dad would do bath-time, cleaning teeth and bedtime story. This gives kids a chance to experience reading, expressing and various fun things in different ways from different people. Recent research has suggested that when fathers read to their under-five-year-old children the children have better language abilities by age four years. There are benefits for children experiencing different parenting skills to let them know that not everybody is the same.

Being a better father and feeling that they're being a better father means committing the time and showing affection, such as being able to give children a hug or having them sit on your lap or snuggle with you, giving them a good night kiss and cuddle or telling them to have a good day at school or at child-care. Of course, if you and your partner are separated, the men in the men's behaviour change program are going to be encouraged to do things that are in the best interests of the children, for example, being consistent when they have visiting times, and making sure they turn up so that the children are not kept waiting or scared that Dad's not coming. After all, they're usually dressed and ready for Dad to turn up and if he doesn't they get terribly disappointed.

As a parent, if your ex-partner is not living with you and the children, a responsible parent would contribute financially by paying regular child support. They will also use the time they have with the children wisely, so it's enjoyable for the children and memorable for the children.

If you're separated, there's an expectation that the father would speak positively about the mother in front of the children and this will be reflected in the men's behaviour change program. The program will also encourage him to think of the children, to talk about the children. So, if you're together and he comes home from the group and he's talked about the effects on the children or parenting of the children, it is hoped that your partner is going to engage more. Maybe he'll ask the children about their day or their progress in school, ask them about their well-being, how they're progressing with friendships, or sport, or other interests.

When domestic and family violence happens in the home the effects on the children can be really negative. Some of the objections that people have may be, "Oh yes we argued but the children were asleep". Really? Did you have time between arguments to go and check? Some people may have, but many may not. The children may have woken momentarily and if you were arguing and it was loud, children can hear.

People will sometimes say, "Well the kids were at their grandparents' house". However, when the kids returned from the grandparents' house they may see your reaction on their return, your longer-term reaction to what occurred in their absence. They may see that you're not talking with each other, that you're more upset, that you're not your happy bubbly self that you were when you dropped them off at their grandparents' house. They may see that you've been crying or that you still seem slightly frustrated, upset, or annoyed. They may see a certain look in their father's eye or a mood that is all too familiar, which means they must go to bed and mind their own business. They quickly learn that they can't ask about domestic violence so they keep their questions and concerns to themselves.

You may be thinking that your kids are babies and that they don't understand, or the kids are adults and of course they understand. Regardless of age, teenagers, children, and babies are affected by domestic and family violence. They can hear what's going on; even if they can't speak, they can get scared. If they're really young, they can feel the tension. If there's repeated domestic and family violence children may develop anxiety and stress: "I hope Mummy's OK, I hope Daddy's not in trouble, I hope they're not fighting, I hope they'll be happy when I get home from school" and that can reduce their concentration and their learning ability.

It can also have long-term effects. For example, when the children are adults and have left home, they may be more likely to accept or engage in domestic and family violence with their partners because they observed it with their parents.

Lundy Bancroft has extensively studied domestic and family violence and the effects on children. His list of emotional effects of domestic and family violence on children show the reality of what can occur for children living in a situation where domestic and family violence has occurred.

Emotional effects on children

Worry, nervousness, fear
Sadness, in worst cases suicidal thoughts
Insecurity
Guilt, self-blame
Anger, resentment
Embarrassment, shame, ceasing inviting friends to their house
Increased responsibility to protect their siblings
Worries about other family members' safety
Worry about, and need to protect, Mum
Blame and resentment towards Mum
Blame and resentment towards siblings
Desire for the power Dad is yielding
Fantasy to stand up to him, and assault or even kill him
Worry about arguing in case the argument turns scary
Uncertainty about what is real

Behavioural effects on children

Bullying, insulting or physical aggression towards friends
Withdrawal from friends
Fear of separation, especially from Mum
Oppositional and defiant behaviours, especially with Mum, but maybe with authority
Regression, for example, bed wetting or accidents during the day
Hyperactivity, hypervigilance, anxiety, obsessive compulsive behaviours
Reduced concentration and learning at school
Overeating or refusing to eat
Sleep problems, for example, nightmares, delayed sleep, waking easily
Violence towards siblings
Failure to thrive in young infants
Running away from home

Adolescent behaviours following domestic and family violence

Substance abuse, for example, caffeine, nicotine, alcohol, or illicit drugs
Poor friendship choices
Violence or verbal abuse towards dating partners, and/or perpetrating sexual assault
Violence or verbal abuse *from* dating partners, and/or sexual victimization
Violence towards Mum

Physically or verbally intervening to protect Mum
Imitating the abuser's behaviour towards Mum

As you read through these lists you may be thinking that you know all of this; after all, you're a mother. But these lists are a reminder that domestic and family violence should not be minimised in terms of its effects on children. Adults can get over fights and even assaults, but children are yet to become adults and have even less choice than you may think you have in your relationship.

These lists are also a good place to return to if your partner attempts to minimise the effects on your children. Try not to get drawn into minimisation of the very real effects on children, both now and into their future. Check on your children, and if they are suffering with these symptoms, they may need a referral to a psychologist or counsellor where it should be safe for them to talk about their worries and concerns. If this is the case, talk with your GP about a referral for your child.

Positive activity

1. Think of a time when your partner was with your children and you were watching from afar, seeing them playing well together. Hold that thought. What were your thoughts when you saw them playing with each other? What were your feelings?

2. Think of a time you did this all together, you and your partner and your children, all playing together, no arguments, having a nice fun time together as a family.

A CHANGE FOR THE BETTER

3. How can you both get back to that special place? What has to happen? Ideally at least one person needs to change, and if you feel you've put a lot of effort in and it's now your partner's time to try to make some change (and that's why he's attending this program), hopefully you're both taking the time to accept and learn aspects of the program that will take you back to that special place where you're all enjoying spending time together and enjoying life together as a family. If you don't have children, the same can apply to the time you and your partner enjoy together as a couple.

CHAPTER 10

DOING IT TOGETHER: SAME LEVEL...EQUAL

Equality is the soul of liberty; there is, in fact, no liberty without it.

— *Frances Wright*

While your partner is learning to take responsibility for his actions, you can both start to share responsibility together. This is all about equality, feeling equal, neither of you being above or better than the other. It is not about extreme feminism where women are believing they can do what men do, or that they don't need men, this is about you being a female, him being a male and you both having equal rights in the relationship. There may be some things that he can do better and there may be some things that you can do better. There are some things that he might be able to do that you can't do, for example those things that may require great strength, and certainly some things

A CHANGE FOR THE BETTER

that you can do that he can't do, for example, getting pregnant and giving birth.

You can remind each other that you both share responsibility. If you don't have children you share the responsibility of earning an income to pay for the domestic situation, paying for a house, either rent or paying off a home loan or setting money aside for renovating your house, or even just the costs of living together, having holidays together or planning social activities. You're doing things together in your relationship, you're both contributing the household in physical or economical ways, and with your ideas of how to decorate your house, where to put the furniture, when to upgrade the garden or yard, or do renovations. You're doing it together.

Try to acknowledge him when he gets it right. Hopefully he'll be doing the same to you. Role model positive behaviour and communication, and let him know you're doing so. This would not be unusual to say, "I've been trying really hard to give you a compliment every day and to notice some of the changes you've made. I'm seeing some change and it's nice." Doing it respectfully, giving him positive feedback about the changes you may be witnessing, is a good way to advance your communication with each other. If he doesn't get it, if he doesn't start following your lead, you may need to re-assess your situation.

One thing that can happen when women have been through domestic and family violence is that it can be very hard to be nice to the man who has harmed you or your children, especially since he's probably been particularly nasty. It can be hard to say nice things, to trust, to be respectful – it can be very hard. Remind yourself that you made a choice to stay together, or that you still have contact if you're not living together.

DOING IT TOGETHER: SAME LEVEL...EQUAL

If he takes responsibility for his actions, it would be good if you can take responsibility for your actions too. Because if he does and you don't, is that fair? It's likely you'll both have different responsibilities. His might be to be honest and kind, and leave the house if he can't do so. Yours might be to be patient and try to trust him, and if this is hard for you, to let him know it's hard. It might seem like small things that you're both doing, but it can be useful to start with small steps.

Is there a way that you can encourage him to continue attending the program?

We've seen in the statistics that the longer the program, the more likelihood of change in the men who attend the full program. The current program that he's attending, if it's the Duluth Program, is typically a 27-week program and in Australia a lot of the government-funded programs are funded for 20 weeks, so it's already a reduction in the number of sessions compared to other successful programs. But 20 weeks is still a considerable commitment of time for him to be showing up, attending, taking in, and processing the information, during and between sessions, and that's a strong commitment for him. Not as big a being in a relationship with you or fathering and parenting children, but it's still a big commitment that is important for him, your relationship and your family.

Part of being on the same level is feeling equal. If you're feeling full from eating a big lunch and he wants a great big evening meal, are you able to say "I just need a small meal for dinner" and let him know you don't necessarily want to cook a big meal? Can you tell him that if he wants a big meal then he can cook? On the other hand, would he be prepared to have something smaller and a bigger meal tomorrow night when you haven't been out for a big lunch? Assertive communication helps with equality. It's about him hearing you and both of you coming to a decision together, problem-solving together and at least trying to involve each other in the decision-making.

Being equal is not about feminism, it's about being respectful, being heard, being understood, being consulted, and feeling like you're on the same level. One gender is not better than the other, they're both wonderful and make up our human race. Having the connection you're having and being as equal as possible can bring about harmony, love, peace, and happiness in a relationship which we, as human beings, are designed to be able to achieve.

Try answering these questions:

1. What can you bring the relationship that your partner doesn't bring? Do you have a special skill, that even with years of training he may not be able to perfect to the extent that you have? Whether that is cooking, playing an instrument, or art, or singing – something that you really enjoy, and that you enjoy sharing with him.

2. Is there something that he is skilled in that you're not an expert in, and even with years of training you may not be able to perfect to the level at which he holds?

3. What is there that you both do together that you both fully enjoy, that you can both practice together, that brings you both closer together, and complements your relationship or your marriage?

4. Share your answers together.

CHAPTER 11

ACTUALLY TALKING

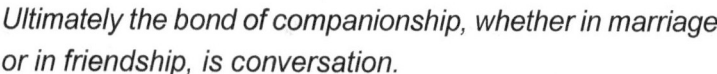

Ultimately the bond of companionship, whether in marriage or in friendship, is conversation.

— *Oscar Wilde*

Communication is key to every relationship. Human beings are the only living things that have the ability to generate verbal communication and discussion. Not even parrots or cockatoos that can mimic human communication can do this. This is about a being that can have thoughts, formulate them into words, and speak the words to another human being, who will then understand what has been said, and reply.

Communication can be friendly, but it can also become quite intimate. Human beings can have intimate communication, communication that is so close, maybe deeply emotional, maybe very personal communication, that they've never had with another person, and this typically occurs in an intimate, loving, relationship.

A CHANGE FOR THE BETTER

Communication should be respectful. We'd hope it's respectful towards the other person in an intimate relationship, just as it should be in any form of relationship. It can also be fun! It's a way to release things to make you feel better or to share excitement and celebration, enjoy good times together, and talk about it along the way. Remembering or reminiscing about good times is a fun activity as well.

As a contrast, refraining from talking, withholding communication, not speaking to your partner, or deliberately ignoring them, is actually emotional abuse. It can also come under the title of passive-aggressive behaviour.

A person doing this might say to you or to themselves, "I'm not shouting at you, I'm not swearing, in fact I'm not even speaking so therefore I'm not being abusive". In actual fact, it is abuse, because the person on the receiving end of the 'silent treatment' is likely to be thinking, "Oh my goodness, I'm being punished. When will they talk with me again? When will we be able to have some nice conversations? This feels emotionally painful, I'm being ignored by my intimate or romantic partner who's supposed to love me."

There is an exception to this, which is the act of being together positively in silence, as this can be a way of communicating togetherness through connection, especially if you're both in agreement that this is a way of enjoying each other's company. An example might be if you're both engaging in a project building something or doing gardening or renovating, where you're both working side by side, not talking but doing an activity together, respecting each other's skills. It's being engaged together and can be a very positive connection with your partner. Other examples of positive silent behaviours might be sharing the same reading time, or silent meditation, or attending a silent meditation retreat together.

ACTUALLY TALKING

Ignoring or refusing to speak is passive-aggressive behaviour, which is where a person is not shouting, not swearing, not being nasty, but they may be using sarcasm. They may be using humour at the other person's expense, such as mimicking you. They may be ignoring or refusing to speak or answer questions, or they may be creating some high level of drama that is over-accentuating their mood and is not a genuine presentation.

Often people will be very hurt from passive-aggressive behaviour. The person dishing it out may think they're defending themselves, saying they have not abused you in any way, but they have.

Think of the last time you really enjoyed talking with your partner. Where were you? How were you feeling? What did you believe would happen as a result of you both talking together?

You may have some objections around communication being key to every relationship, if your partner has not been talkative during your relationship or marriage. These may include: "He won't talk, it's not him, he's not a talker, he's never been a talker". I would then ask how he talked with you when you first met? Did you do all the talking? How did he commit to you? Whether it was marriage or moving in together in a relationship. How did he communicate that to you?

You may hand over some of your personal power to him, so you may be letting him make all the decisions, even what you eat and what you both buy, or what you might order at a restaurant, allowing him to order for you. For some people it's romantic or exciting to have their partner order their food for them.

I'm sure you can think of a time when he didn't make all the decisions. Part of the decision to start a relationship was yours at the beginning of the relationship. You might state that "We don't like talking because there's no time. He gets up early and leaves for work, and when he gets home I'm cooking the dinner and getting the children to bed, or he is doing that, and we don't have time to talk, then we go to bed and we're too tired to do anything but sleep".

My suggestion to someone who is claiming they have no time to talk: Make time! Talking is an act of intimacy. It's respectful and it shows mutual respect so it's equal. He respects you and you respect him, you're planning, you're reminiscing, reminding each other of fun times you've had together, you may be talking about how your day has been or how you'd like your evening to be. This is particularly important for maintaining a good relationship.

Making time

Actions you can take to make time include:

Set aside a time to talk. This may be on a Sunday at the end of the week because Saturday might be sport day or shopping day, or visiting family day, so Sundays can sometimes be a free day, either having breakfast, brunch, or lunch. The children can be playing, and you can both take some time to talk together.

Make use of the night. When your children have gone to bed at night, you could take time to sit down in your lounge or living room and talk. Can you set an earlier bedtime for your children? Or, when you both go to bed try suggesting: "Let's not go to sleep straight away, let's give each other five minutes (or longer) each to talk about our day, or state one, or more, good things that happened during the day".

ACTUALLY TALKING

Make use of the morning. Plan time in the morning when you wake up, having a cup of tea, coffee, or breakfast together, and a quick chat. Remember it's about quality not quantity.

Set a time limit. If you have a busy lifestyle, set a time, for example one hour, and set the time on the weekend. Try to stick to that one hour so it doesn't take two or three hours and you find you didn't get everything done that you'd usually do on a weekend and then resent spending the time talking. Make it an enjoyable time. If neither of you are working and you have time, and you're not having to attend to children, there's no need for a time limit. Make sure that it remains enjoyable though, as we can lose concentration, people can get irritable and can lose interest in taking altogether. Be guided by your partner's, and your own, attention span, desire for talk, and comfort. Some people don't like to sit still for long, so talking could be during a walk or a drive, or another activity.

Make it a regular time. If you don't get to talk to each other during the week, and you have a regular time planned, for example, every Sunday, then you'll know you can raise it at your specified talking time. Write down a list of things you'd like to talk about, and then talk about them at your scheduled time. Try to stick to your schedule. If you miss it one week, come back to it the next week. For others who have a lot to talk about you might to allocate that time a bit more regularly than once a week, it might be once a day or every other day. Spice it up and plan your talk over dinner at a restaurant or your favourite eating place.

Communication needs to be positive. Try to keep all communication positive, meaningful and respectful, with equal time unless one person has little to talk about and they're happy for the other person to talk more. But try to have equal time to speak, and being heard.

The talking time needs to be confidential, not discussed later or broadcast to family members, unless you both agree to have an open communication style that is accepted as being discussed outside your relationship; however, intimate relationships are about intimacy, and there are often secrets. They typically don't include telling family and friends about your intimate situations, thoughts or ideas, depending on your topic, for example, planning a holiday versus regularity of having sex. Make sure you confirm your level of private communication and respect each other's wishes.

We know that people who talk and communicate in a positive, respectful, and productive manner with, not to, their partner, are putting the work into maintaining the longevity of their relationship. Make it fun, make it enjoyable not overbearing, end each communication time with something positive, a compliment or encouragement, and a reminder of positive feelings you may have for each other, for example, "I enjoyed our talk", "Thanks for listening", "Thanks for sharing", "Thanks for joining me", "Thanks for caring" or "Thanks for being you".

If it's too hard to talk together, it might be helpful to engage in relationship counselling or therapy, where approaching certain topics can be done in a safe environment, and encouragement to communicate positively can be suggested to your partner by an experienced person who will guide you both into using positive communication again and offer suggestions and tips for enhancing your communication with each other.

The 12 Steps of Change

When your partner has completed his men's behaviour change program it would be reasonable for you to expect that he has made

ACTUALLY TALKING

some, if not all, of the following changes as suggested by Bancroft, Silverman and Ritchie (2012):

1. He has fully disclosed the history of physical and psychological violence towards you and any children you may have.
2. He recognises that his actions are unacceptable.
3. He recognises that his actions were chosen.
4. He recognises and shows empathy for the effects of his actions on you and your children.
5. He recognises the patterns of his controlling behaviours and entitled attitudes.
6. He has developed respectful behaviours and attitudes.
7. He has re-evaluated his distorted image of you (especially those he held at the times of violence).
8. He has made amends in the short and long-term.
9. He has accepted the consequences of his actions for him.
10. He has committed to not repeating the abusive behaviour.
11. He has accepted change as a long-term, even life-long, process.
12. He is willing to be accountable.

A conversation with your partner about these 12 steps of change would be a good place to practice positive communication, actually talking, especially if you have relatively good communication skills already. If the conversation becomes too emotional, leave it for another time. You can monitor these changes and use them as a guide for yourself and your views of your partner's change. Not all men will have completed all 12 steps. This is a guide and can be an ongoing behaviour change project or means of monitoring, observation, or discussion. Remember that change can take time and can be hard to discuss.

A CHANGE FOR THE BETTER

How did Nate, Jack, and Chris go with their 12 steps?

Please note that these 12 steps are not a scoring system for participants in the groups, but merely the writer's license to complete the stories of the scenario characters in this book.

Nate

If we were scoring the three men in the scenarios, we'd see that Nate scored 12 out of 12. He grasped the concepts and made changes to his thoughts, feelings, behaviours, and beliefs and accepted all 12 steps. He has been spreading the word to others in his friendship circle, and, due to his contributions in the group, he was invited to sign up to volunteer with future men's groups, with the option of training to become a co-facilitator. He didn't accept this offer because his first commitment after completing the 20-week group program was to take Natalia on a camping trip that they'd both dreamed of when they first met. He was putting the relationship with Natalia first and choosing to spend time with her doing something she had asked to do, an activity they both enjoy together.

Jackson

Jackson would have scored 6 out of 12. He had fully disclosed the history of physical and psychological violence towards Olivia. He recognised that his actions were unacceptable. He recognised that his actions were chosen. But he didn't make change initially. When Olivia decided to leave him, he finally accepted the consequences of his actions for his behaviour. He accepted change as a long-term, even life-long, process, and he eventually became willing to be accountable. Better late than never, but not a positive journey for Olivia.

Chris

Chris scored 2 out of 12. He fully disclosed the history of physical and psychological violence towards his ex-partner. He did not fully disclose his current behaviours towards Emily. He accepted that his actions were chosen, and he chose to do what he wanted. That didn't include attending to his partner or trying to listen to the concepts taught in the group, and of course, he re-offended and ceased attending.

CHAPTER 12

WHAT IF HE RELAPSES?

If a partner is controlling, abusive, and violent in the kitchen, the living room, and in public, why would he stop the abuse at the bedroom door?

— Hon. Jeffrey Kremers

Back to the DV cycle

Is it a lapse or a relapse if domestic and family violence occurs again in your relationship? If it's a lapse, it only occurs again once. If this happens, ask yourself if you are prepared to wait around to see if it happens again? Is it safe for you to do so?

If the lapse is physical or sexual violence it is an assault and is against the law as it places your life in danger. This sort of lapse is definitely unacceptable, and if it happens it would be important for you to take action.

A CHANGE FOR THE BETTER

This is something that would be good to talk through with another person, to get another point of view, because if domestic and family violence has occurred again to you then this is a time where you do need to stay safe and make a decision about your life.

The main difference between a lapse and a relapse is that a lapse is a one-off incident of the behaviour occurring again, in this case domestic and family violence, whereas a relapse is when a person returns immediately to the behaviour that was occurring on a regular basis. It is not a one-off situation.

What does this mean for you? In your mind, there may be extenuating circumstances as to why this occurred. For example, you may feel that your partner has tried to keep his cool and his reaction was not as big as usual; it may be that in the past he's used physical violence and this time it was verbal violence. This is still not OK, but it could be a different presentation from the past. He might still be 'trying'. This is something that you need to weigh up with somebody else without minimising the situation, as often victims do. Any lapse is not OK, it's still domestic and family violence.

You have a choice about your life, you have a choice as to whether you act on this lapse from your partner. It is your life that you can make decisions about. Ultimately this is about your safety. If this is a lapse or relapse of your partner going back to domestic and family violence cycle by committing domestic and family violence again and knowing there may be an ultimatum, then your safety is paramount. If he has had an outburst and been violent and realised that you may choose to end the relationship once and for all, you would benefit from support straight away. If he thinks you're leaving "because he stuffed up again" his behaviour could escalate, and you're probably not safe.

WHAT IF HE RELAPSES?

Your safety is always the number one priority, and that includes the children, because you are going to be in charge of the children. If you can imagine the scenario of owning a pet and realising that there's smoke in your house. You have to protect yourself, cover your airways, assess the situation, assess the safety of saving your cat or dog, or send the fire brigade in to save the cat or dog.

In the case of domestic and family violence you have to assess the situation, just like being on an airplane where you're told, in the case of an emergency, to put your oxygen mask on first before helping your children to put theirs on. Look after yourself first then look after your children.

The hypothetical scenario characters

Nate, Jackson, and Chris are all human beings, based on real characters. They all made choices, and they all deserve to be who they choose to be. That doesn't mean you have to choose to like them or support their actions. You can make decisions about who you like, who you trust, and who you want to share your life with.

The risks are high at the end of any relationship. If you are planning to end your relationship, you must address your safety. **Your safety plan** is your means of staying safe or even staying alive.

Your quality of life is important. You should be able to enjoy your life, and your family must be safe and happy. If you're enjoying your relationship and you have a say in what happens in your relationship and your life, then you're both on the right track.

If you are not enjoying your life, if domestic and family violence continues and your quality of life is not positive or at a high level, it may be time to re-think or re-assess your situation, and the same goes for your children. Do they have a good quality of life, are they happy? Or are they running away from violence, shouting, swearing, or copying their father's behaviour? Are their lives fulfilling and positive? Are they comfortable and safe enough to play and learn while having fun and enjoying relationships.

Try to focus on the present, not on the past. Your situation may have been positive at the beginning of your relationship but now you may be going through distress. Is this something that you and your family need to discuss, even your extended family? Is this a time to consult your extended family, whether it's your parents or your partner's parents or your friends, to discuss what's going on for you in your life? Don't confuse this with intimate information. If your safety is at stake and you are leaving a relationship or calling the police, you may need to disclose personal aspects of the abuse you have endured.

If you're not sure what to do:

1. Talk to a friend, one you can confide in about personal matters. Try not to focus on saying negative things about your partner, but try to focus on your situation and how his actions make you feel, or talk about your day-to-day life, and what you need to be doing, but may feel held back from. Are you being impacted and not able to go to work, do what you need to be doing – be that activities or other responsibilities – or focus on you, your well-being and your safety? It will help to talk about these factors.

2. Call the women's advocate if your partner is in a men's behaviour change program, and you have access to the women's advocate. You could also talk to a counsellor or

WHAT IF HE RELAPSES?

your GP, who may refer you to a psychologist. You could talk to the Domestic & Family Violence Prevention Centre (DFVPC), or call the 1800 Respect line.

3. Take another look at the DV cycle. Where are things for you and your partner on the DV cycle right now?

4. Have another look at the stage of changes. Where is your partner in terms of change? Where are they for you?

5. If you're planning to leave, take someone with you when you tell your partner. Stay safe. Be aware of the risks and take precautions. **Revisit your safety plan** and **seek support** as recommended.

Actions for relapse:

1. Talk with someone. If things are not going well, try to talk with someone every day. If things are bad or there's been a lapse or relapse to physical or sexual violence, call the police, and call an ambulance if you've been injured, or get someone else to call for you. Call the 1800 Respect line or the Domestic and Family Violence Prevention Centre in your area as they can give detailed tips about what your actions can be on the day. Call your parents, even if you don't feel you have a great relationship with them. Call your siblings. Reach out to people. People enjoy helping others. If you reach out to them it'll make them feel good to come and help you.

2. Stay safe. It is vitally important for you to stay safe and help the children in the house to stay safe, as well as others who may be present, for example other adults. Whether

that means you have to shut yourself in a room, have to go out of the house, or call 000, just stay safe.

3. Protect your children. But first, put your 'oxygen mask' on. Have a think about all the times that your partner may have said to you "You need help". Start thinking about tactfully saying that to him. If he is continuing to engage in domestic and family violence towards you, then you do need help, but appropriate help.

Think about him taking responsibility, and that may be about him attending another domestic and family violence intervention program to learn about his sense of entitlement, coercion and control over you which has resulted in him engaging in domestic and family violence. He is the main person that needs help to change this damaging behaviour. If the domestic and family violence continues to increase someone will call the police. It may not be you, it may be neighbours hearing noises or shouting coming from your house. The worst case scenario may be that he ends up in jail and won't have access to the children or you, and the family is broken up.

Rather than getting to that stage, look at prevention rather than cure, including him, and allowing him to include you in learning different thoughts, beliefs and actions to prevent any relapses of domestic and family violence in your relationship.

Keep in touch with your beliefs and your views of the DV cycle. It is acknowledged that some women practice leaving a relationship, or asking their partner to leave the relationship, taking a weekend away to see what it's like, spending a night or two away from their partner as a trial. Then it might be a week or two longer next time, to see how it feels for you, before you take the final step towards a permanent separation.

WHAT IF HE RELAPSES?

You can get used to living with a partner if you've been together for a long time, so spending time apart can feel very different. Practicing short periods apart can be helpful, unless the violence is really bad and you need to be away and stay away, or have him removed from the house so that you have safety for yourself and your children.

Remember that the DV cycle can be a revolving door and people can go around and around this cycle until someone makes a firm decision. That someone may be you. It may be you dealing with your issues and leaving your partner to deal with his issues, or it could be police or a magistrate or judge making that decision for you.

On the other hand, you could continue to plant the seed of what it is that you believe your partner needs to do to make himself a better man for a better relationship for you and your family and for society in general.

Best wishes for a safe and positive relationship with your partner, and if that doesn't happen, engage and connect with your friends, family, and supports to avoid any return to the domestic violence cycle. Relationships should be safe, loving, and respectful for both people involved. I hope this is the case for you.

AFTERWORD

Now that you've read this book, keep it handy in case you want to re-read sections that may be referred to in future conversations with your partner or family member about their men's behaviour change group attendance. Don't give the book to a friend just yet.

If you know a woman who's experiencing domestic and family violence, try to be there to support them, give them the referral options, be their friend and part of their safety network if you can. If their matter goes to court, or if children are impacted and engaged with children's services, support this woman and her children, as most women do, and encourage the man to take responsibility by attending a men's behaviour change program.

When he starts attending the program, rather than giving your female friend your copy, tell him to purchase a copy of this book for his partner or family member. After all, this book is a symbol of his commitment to her, his choice to take responsibility, practice equality, and non-violence, and make a change for the better.

ABOUT THE AUTHOR

Amanda Akers was born in Sydney and raised her first two children in the Eastern Suburbs. During the 90s she moved to Armidale in the New England region of NSW where she furthered her study, worked in the public and private sector, and had her third child.

Amanda has worked as a Clinical Psychologist in the drug and alcohol field, which included providing outreach services to smaller towns outside Armidale and running psycho-education programs. She had begun her career as a telephone counsellor in Sydney, which was voluntary work that she later pursued in Armidale, working for telephone counselling services such as Careline and Bush Support Services, as well as after-hours on-call services for the crisis sexual assault service. In Armidale, Amanda ran her own private practice: New England Psychological Services.

Amanda relocated to the Gold Coast to enjoy the warmer weather and opened a new practice, Akers Psychology, where she continued to provide therapy, conduct psychological and forensic assessments, run workshops in rural and remote locations, while she has also presented papers at conferences across Australia. In

2024, Amanda moved back to Armidale, New South Wales, where she continues to operate Akers Psychology offering face-to-face and telehealth services.

Amanda is a Member of the Australian Psychological Society (APS) and a Fellow of the APS College of Clinical Psychologists. She has contributed to the APS as a Committee Member of Interest Groups, and contributes to the profession of psychology by supervising Intern Clinical Psychologists and providing supervision to rural and remote psychologists and allied health workers. She provides guest lectures to universities in the field of psychology and rural and remote work. She has been a Board Member of Lifeline New England, and Member of the Steering Committee for the refurbishment of Freeman House Drug and Alcohol Rehabilitation Centre, in Armidale, and Chaired a Management Committee for a centre for sexual assault victims in the New England Region.

Amanda's concerns for the well-being and safety of family members of drug users prompted her to write her first book, *Frozen Families: 7 Essentials for Survival When You Have an Ice User in Your Life*. Her second book: *Let's Have a Clean Conversation*, is not drug-specific but encourages readers to speak openly and positively about drug rehabilitation options with their partners or family members who use drugs.

Amanda has a keen interest in equity groups, rural and remote issues, and the drug and alcohol field. Her interests also include domestic and family violence, and she is a qualified co-facilitator of men's behaviour change programs. Her interest in domestic and family violence prompted her to write this book for the female partners of men attending men's behaviour change programs, to ensure they feel included and knowledgeable about the process of change in their partner or family member.

AMANDA AS A GUEST SPEAKER

Amanda Akers is a Clinical Psychologist with extensive experience working in the areas of drugs and alcohol, and domestic and family violence. She provides guest lectures from community to university level, including in rural and remote locations. She engages face-to-face or online with individuals or groups about relevant drug and alcohol issues, domestic and family violence, anxiety, depression, and other psychological presentations.

Amanda has worked in metropolitan and rural communities and acknowledges the challenges faced by individuals, families, and communities when drugs and alcohol and/or domestic and family violence take over people's lives. She works to assist people to find the cognitive, behavioural, and communication skills to maintain safety and to find solutions to issues that disrupt the harmony of life that we all deserve.

Contact Info:
Akers Psychology
Ph: 07 5519 9668
M: 0411 247 549
amanda@akerspsychology.com.au
www.akerspsychology.com.au

A CHANGE FOR THE BETTER

Amanda is a sought-after guest speaker on the following topics:

Ice use, abuse, and treatment	Staying safe, reducing the impact of ice-fuelled interactions, accessing support or treatment for families and ice users, or other drug users
General drug and alcohol education	Alcohol, drugs (including nicotine), treatment options
Managing anxiety	Cognitive and behavioural management of anxiety, treatment options
Managing depression	Cognitive and behavioural management of depression, treatment options
Resilience in difficult situations	Positive and assertive communication, reflective practice, and self-care
Positive ageing	Acceptance of all levels of ageing in a positive manner
Domestic and family violence education	Men's behaviour change programs, staying safe, referral options
Other related topics	By direct application

NOTES

A CHANGE FOR THE BETTER

NOTES

www.ingramcontent.com/pod-product-compliance
Lightning Source LLC
Chambersburg PA
CBHW050254120526
44590CB00016B/2352